I Am Patrick
A Donegal Childhood Remembered

by Patrick Doherty

I Am Patrick
A Donegal Childhood Remembered

By Patrick Doherty

Clachan Publishing
26 Rathlin Road, Ballycastle,
Glens of Antrim, BT54 6AQ

Email: clachanpublishing@outlook.com
Website: http://clachanpublishing-com.
ISBN: 978-1-909906-58-7

Copyright © Patrick Doherty

ALL RIGHTS RESERVED.

This book contains material protected under International Copyright Laws and Treaties. Any unauthorised reprint, sale or use of this material is prohibited. No part of this book may be reproduced or transmitted in any form or by any means, electronic or mechanical, including photocopying, recording, or by any information storage and retrieval system without express written permission from the author / publisher.

Clachan Publishing

GLOSSARY

aise	Ease.
amadan	A fool.
auld	Old.
binch	A bench.
bink	The vertical face of the turf plot.
brae	A low hill or slope.
camogie	A team game played by women in Ireland using a small ball and a stick.
carageen moss	A red, algae grown on rocks used to make sauces.
céad míle fáilte	Irish for 'welcome'.
corphouse	The Irish three days' wake in the home.
crater	A poor little creature.
creel	A large wicker basket.
disc cutter	A machine with two rows of metal discs attached to the back of a tractor flat for chopping lumpy soil.
drooked	Drenched.
dulse	Edible seaweed.
ESB	The Electricity Supply Board.
futen	Standing three pieces of wet turf in a conical shape.
graip	A four-pronged fork.
hames	A pair of curved metal tubes around a horse's collar.
harrow	A spiked, flat, wooden frame dragged over soil to break it up.
hauld yir wisht	Be quiet.
hoor	Whore.
juke	To bend low.
kerry	To carry.
kerry on	To continue.

make right hames of it	To make a mess of something.
oxter	Armpit.
peoreens	Small potatoes.
pirties	Potatoes.
pit	A heap of potatoes.
planter	A machine attached to the back of a tractor for planting potatoes.
riddle skip	A waist-high wooden frame holding two metal meshes of different sizes to separate potatoes.
rodeen	A path.
sally rod	A thin branch from the weeping willow tree used for punishing children.
scutch grass	Long thick grass.
shuch	An open drain.
skip	A waist-high wooden frame to put potatoes on.
slat mara	Seaweed used for fertilising soil.
splits	Potatoes cut for planting.
St.Brigid's cross	A cross made from rushes to celebrate the Feast of St.Brigid on 1st February.
stooks	Four sheaves of corn in a conical shape.
tauld	Told.
wan(s)	One.
whin	Gorse.

In Memoriam

Cahir Doherty

1948-2014

Acknowledgements

Thank you to Catharine Frances for her support throughout the writing of this memoir.

Thank you to Frank McGuinness, Donegal-born poet, and playwright, for his very kind permission for the use of the poems *Malin Head* and *Clay*.

Contents

Glosssary i

Cleaning Corn 2
Granddad 4
Running Home 12
Brendan 19
Driving to Carnryan 24
Sacraments 25
The 15th 32
Docks 39
Corn 40
Quiggy 47
Woodbines 61
The Border 70
Potatoes 72
Pythagoras 82
Ploughing 85
Veni, vidi… 87
Turf 91
Troubles 98
Algebra 99
Going Home 102
Cheating 104
The Sound of Music 107
Inishowen 115
Interview 116
Malin Head 121
Cahir 124

Mooney's Bar	128
The Corphouse	137
Teacher Training	139
Sheila	141
The Star of the Sea	144
À Harfleur	148
First Post	154
Lagg	157
First Day	161

Patrick Doherty grew up in Malin Head, Ireland's most northerly point. He attended Colgan Hall in Carndonagh, Donegal and later trained to be a French teacher in Manchester. He taught French and was a headteacher in Lancashire schools for more than thirty years. Patrick now lives in France.

Malin Head

This is as far as this country takes you.
Ireland ends here, rocks like rams' pointed horns.
The ocean's magnet, it pulls you northwards.

And the rocks, the ram, they look for the blue,
the red intoxicating stain of born
and being. This place, Malin Head is hard.

I wish I could let you walk this landscape.
It has no fear of death. It invites flight,
Gyrfalcon, my beautiful gyrfalcon,

you, my rock, my ram, my Malin Head, son
of the moon eclipsed by earth, my red night,
in my head tonight I think I will cope.

I'll go to my sleep and dream at my ease.
I wish all you wish, I wish you reason.

Frank McGuinness *The Stone Jug*

Cleaning Corn

The fans in the barn start to tirn. Daddy an James must be cleanen corn. I hear Daddy taalken. I want him to talk to me. Chaff flies through the door. I'm not allowed near the fans. I step nearer. They lift a bag of corn on tap of the fans. The corn bounces down lake hailstones. I want to tirn the big metal handle. I cud make the fans roar. When Daddy's not lucken I grab it. I pull it. I ken't move it. It lucks aisy when he does it. I pull harder. It starts to move. The cogs begin to tirn. When the handle reaches the tap I hev to let go a it. I catch it agen as it comes down. I pull. The small cog goes faster than the big cog. I let go a the handle as it reaches the tap agen. I step closer to see how the cogs work. Lumps a grease stick to them. I poke it. The cogs squash the end a me finger. I scream. The handle hits me head. James grabs me an runs towards the kitchen. 'What the hell wur ye doen?' Me hand shivers. I ken't see me fingernail. A red lump hangs aff. Blood trickles to me elbow and onto the ground.

'Oh, Jesus, Mary and Joseph. What's happened?' Mammy shouts.
'Mammy, Mammy. His finger. He might a lost it, the little crater.'
'Oh God bless us and save us.'
'Hold it up. Higher, Patrick. Higher,' grabben a cloth. She wraps it round me finger. She tells me to haul it up to me chest. She sits me on a chair. I start to shiver. Me teeth chatter.
'What in God's name was he doing near the fans?'
'Don' know. Didn't even know he wuz in there. Thought Daddy wuz on the handle.'
'Tell Daddy to get in here now.'

Not Daddy. Please. She stoops in front of me. Her nose touches mine. 'What have I always told you about machinery?' I stare at her. I wipe me eyes. I know what she's goen to say. I don't answer. 'Stay away.' I remember her words from afore, when she saw me outside. 'Keep away from the tractor. Don't go near the bull. Stay near the house where I can see you.'

Daddy's wellingtons bang the path at the kitchen door. Mammy tirns round. She stares at him. Me hands shake. I slide to the edge of me chair and try to run to me bedroom. He stares at her. Daddy stares at me. I wait for them to speak. 'He cud've lost an arm, you know. Where the hell were you?' her voice tremblen as she wipes her eyes. 'Jesus, Mary and Joseph, I've enough to do.'

Daddy rubs his forehead. I luck down. He flattens his grey hair. He lucks at the blood on the floor. 'Should a take 'im to Dr. Friel?'

Mammy shakes her head an groans as she picks me up. 'His nail's gone,' she cries. Daddy bows his head. I luck down. The tip of my finger is fallen aff.

I am taken to the doctor. Day after day Mammy takes aff the sodden bandage lake the doctor showed her. She haulds me hand up close to her face an tirns me wrist to the window. I squeeze me eyes shut. I try not to cry. 'The blood's drying up. You'll end up losing that nail. The swelling's going down. It'll take that blue skin a long time to heal.'

Mammy dips me finger in Dettol with water added to it. It stings. The jagged edges turn white. She wraps fresh gauze an a soft bandage round it an then a thick leather cover with string round me wrist. When I lower me hand me finger throbs. When I raise it, it throbs. I cup me left hand round it. It still hurts. I rest me hand across me chest in bed. I feel the leather. Me finger stings. I want to open the knot. I want to take the leather aff an see if there's any blood. I won't to be able to tie it agen. I hauld me hand above me head. I turn on me side an roll back. It itches. I want to rub it. I cry.

After a bit Mammy stops putten on the leather cover. I ken move me finger a little. I hold me other hand round it. Each day the swellen goes down. The blood hardens an goes black. A white crust appears round the edge. It starts to curl. The tap of me finger is sliced aff. I ken't see me nail. After the nail appears only half of it grows. It bends sideways. It's soft. I bend me finger into me palm.

,

3

Granddad

Daddy an James kerried the brown settee an two armchairs from the sitten room into Granddad's room yisterday. The room seems bigger. The green an brown carpet lucks new where the settee an chairs were. Round flat dints show where their feet dug into it. A row of chairs stands round the walls. It's darker with the curtains half shut. Mammy lights the two new candles in the silver candle stick holders on the mantelpiece. They flicker on the cream wallpaper. 'What's in that bowl? Mammy?'

'Holy water,' dippen two fingers in an sprinklen it ivrywhere with a flick a her wrist.

'What's that for?'

'Blessing the room before Granddad comes home.'

'Where is he?'

'In hospital.'

'Why?'

'Well, he's been very ill.'

'Why?'

'Just be quiet. Stop asking so many questions, will you. Come with me for some turf.' I kerry the gold-coloured bucket. Mammy fills it from the stack at the side of the barn. 'We need plenty of brown ones to get the fire going. We'll come back for the black pieces to put on top. They're as hard as coal,' she groans as she lifts the bucket.

I jump to grab the handle. She puts it by the fire an lights the crunched up *Derry Journal* covered with brown tirf. 'You stay in the kitchen.'

The gravel in the street rattles. I rush to the liven room window. A big black car reverses up to the gate. 'Mammy, Mammy, there's a big black car here.' She opens the front door. She blesses herself with her rosary beads. Daddy an James stand by the gate. The driver, in a black suit an hat, gets out. He opens the boot. Another man, in a black suit an hat, gets out the other door. 'Good mornen,' says the driver tilten his hat an nodden.

I tiptoe up behind Mammy an hauld her hand. The driver kerries a silver frame with wheels on it. 'Yes, in the sitting room there, Mickey,' as Mammy points to the door. I rush to the window agen. The two men slide a long wooden box out, haulden the end. It has two silver handles on each side. Daddy an James lift the other end. I slide me face along the glass as they enter the hallway. The men disappear. The big box moves in. Daddy an James disappear. I sneak round the sitten room door. They put the box on the silver frame an nod at Mammy.

'What's in the box, Mammy?'

'It's Granddad. He died.'

'Why?' She puts her arms round me shoulders an waalks me to the kitchen. 'It's called a coffin. Stay here. I'll be back shortly,' shutten the door behind her.

Father Kelly arrives. He has a long cloth round his neck, a prayer book an a small bottle in his hand. 'Hello, Father. Come in, Father.'

'Good afternoon, Lizzie. I'm so sorry for your troubles,' wipen his shoes on the wire mat. Mickey an Roger from over the road tirn away from him. They don't lake him because he reads out their names when they don't bring a load a tirf in September or if they don't give him money. He tells all farmers aff if they cut the corn on a Sunday. Some are so angry they go to the chapel in Lagg. Mammy an Daddy don't lake him but they are nice to him because he's helpin Cahir. Mammy wants Cahir to be a priest lake Mrs. Post Office's son, Philip, in Carn Malin.

Cahir says Father Kelly scares him on the altar. I don't want to be an altar boy lake him. I don't lake Father Kelly. After me big brother Willie came home from Chicago, he tauld me Father Kelly hit him across the face on the altar when he didn't kerry the bible properly.

I think a when he came into our classroom an stared at Cathleen sitten next to me. 'Cathleen, who made you?'

'Mammy an Daddy made me, Father.'

Mrs. Monaghan whacks her cane on the table. 'Get outside this minute before I beat you. That'll be her grandmother telling her that, Father. Oh, she's a bad article.'

'Don't you worry, Mrs. Monaghan. I'll go to Mrs. Bannon straightaway.'

Mammy kerries a tray with a pot a tea, milk an sugar. She comes back for the flowery cups an saucers in the glass cupboard. The bottom of the cups is small. The top lucks bigger than the cups in the scullery. They're shiny. I don't remember them bein used afore. I peep through the sitten room door when she goes in.

I think Grandad's ben in the coffin for two days. I'm not allowed in. People come an go between the scullery, kitchen an the sitten room. Some men sit in the kitchen. Other men sit in the liven room. They drink bottles of Guinness an whiskey. I don't lake the smell. Some stand near the front door. They pull their collars up an tighten their caps over their foreheads. They move from fut to fut shruggen their shoulders. Daddy passes round a plate a cigarettes. The wind blows the smoke sideways. Mammy puts her arm round me waist. She pulls me closer. She takes me hand an pulls me from the smoke. 'Your granddad was very old, Patrick. He was ninety-three.'

'What's ninety-three?'

'Look, there's his picture on the wall.' I bend me head back. His face fills the black frame. His cheek rests on his fist. His thumb nail is black. His eyes stare. Bits of white hair lie flat across his head lake Daddy's. Thick black glasses cover his eyebrows. I luck round.

The women luck at me. They say nothen. They sit in a row along the wall. All the women are here an all the men are in the kitchen. Some women have veils over their faces. I ken't make out who they are. Ivrybody lucks auld. I ken't tell who's younger or aulder. They're just auld. I don't want to be auld. They must feel horrible. I ken't understand what some of them are sayen.

Mammy hands a gold tin box of yellow snuff to the women. They pass it to each other. They pinch a little between two fingers an put it on the back of their hand. They put it up to their nose an breathe in. They screw up their faces. Some sneeze. Some rub their eyes. Some take a deep breath. I don't know why they do it. They don't seem to lake it. I want them to empty the box. I lake the shiny smooth tin an round lid.

I wish somewan wud tell me what's goen on. I hardly know anywan. I want to go an play outside but it's wet an cold. Mammy won't let me play inside because the house is full of people. 'Patrick's the baby of the family,' Mammy says to a woman sitten near her.

I put me arm over me face. Dan doesn't want to play because he's aulder. He's in the juniors an I'm in the infants. He's eight. Daddy lets him sit between his knees on the tractor. They hauld the steeren wheel an laugh. I want to do that.

'We're saying the rosary now,' Mammy whispers. She reaches for the rosary beads on the fireplace an sits on her round leather stool. She puts her arm round me. 'We'll say the rosary now', she says in a louder voice to ivrywan. 'In the name of The Father and The Son and The Holy Ghost.' Mammy moves her thumb over the first single bead. The cross wi' Jesus on dangles over her knee. His face lucks down. Twigs lie on his head. A piece of brown thread ties the cross to the chain of beads.

'Why is he on the cross? Why's he got twigs on his head, Mammy?' She frowns an pulls me tighter.

People cough. They stop talken. The men take their caps aff. Some kneel on the floor. Others stamp their cigarettes on the pavement. They make the sign of the cross lake they are waften dung flies away. They fold their arms across their stomach. Ivrybody mumbles. The women bow their heads. Their veils dangle over their faces. They kiss the cross on their rosary beads. They rest their hands on their lap. They rub the beads. Their lips hardly move. They start an finish at different times. They mumble lake the hum of the big drum of the threshen mill in the barn when it turns fast. I know all the words aff by heart from kneelen on the floor ivry night an resten me elbows on the hard chair. I don't understand the words.

'Hail Mary, full of grace.
The Lord is with thee.
Blessed art thou amongst women,
And blessed is the fruit of thy womb, Jesus.' She stops. Ivrybody mumbles.
'Holy Mary, Mother of God,
Pray for us sinners,
Now and at the hour of our death.
Amen.'

I count a bead ivry time she moves her thumb. The black paint is worn through the wood on some beads. I count ten on me fingers. Mammy starts.

'Glory be to the Father and The Son
And the Holy Ghost.' Mammy stops. Ivrybody mumbles.
'As it was in the beginning,
Is now and ever shall be,
World without end,
Amen.'

I shuffle. I rub me eyes. I stand on me toes to reach round Mammy's neck. The lid of the coffin stands against the wall in the corner. I ken't see Granddad. At the end of the rosary she stands up. 'God, you're so heavy now.' She steps towards the coffin. I grip her neck tighter. I hide me face in her neck. The smell of camphor an cow dung make me snort. I luck round. I think it's the men at the front door. The flames from the fire shine on the silver legs under the coffin. Cards stand on the edge. They luck lake they'll faal aff. Mammy picks them up an reads them.

'What's them for, Mammy?'
'Oh, just cards from everybody.'
'Where's his glasses, Mammy?'

His eyebrows luck bigger. His hair is flat. A white sheet covers him up to his neck. His arms rest on tap. His hands are joined together. They hauld his rosary beads tied together with pieces of thread. A tear itches me nose. I bury me head in Mammy's neck. She pats me head. She rubs me back. She carries me into the kitchen. 'Mary, can you warm me a cup of milk for Patrick, please. He's had a long day. Very tantrummy. Mind you I'm so tired too.'

'For God's sake, Lizzie, you're run aff yer feet. Go an rest. I'll sort out Patrick.'

It's eight o'clock. 'It's Granddad's funeral today, Patrick,' Mammy says as she comes into me bedroom. 'Let's get you to the sink for a good wash.' Not the big white sink agen. I'll shiver, sitten on the edge in me underpants. She'll rub the hard, pink carbolic soap on me head, face an neck. It'll hurt. The suds'll sting me eyes. The soapy water'll smell lake Dettol. It'll trickle over me lips. It'll make me feel sick. Me eyes'll be red an sore. She'll tell me aff for rubben them. I cud wash meself lake when she lets me wash me feet afterwards in the sink. I lake playen with the soap when it's soft an warm. It turns a pale pink. I make patterns with me nails an then rub them away.

'Right, get yourself dried. Your suit is on the wardrobe door with the white shirt and red tie.' I go back into the kitchen with the tie in me hand. 'Give it to me,' pullen up me collar an yanken the tie round me neck. She knots it an slides it right up to the tap button. 'Wait while I do your hair.'

I feel I'm choken. I poke me finger inside the collar an loosen it. Mammy returns with her long brown comb and Brycreem. She pats a dollop over me hair, rubs it, combs it an flattens it with her hand. 'Make sure you sit here and wait,' rushen back into the bedroom. She shuts the door. I luck out the window. Men an women waalk in wans and twos along the Carn Malin winden road from Mary Anne's shop to our house. I don't understand why they stand outside our gate. The men have shaved. They wear black suits, ties an clean shoes. They don't smoke. Some women hev veils. Some wear black hats an black gloves.

Daddy goes into the bedroom an shuts the door. Me brothers Willie, John, James, Kevin, Cahir, Dan an me sister, Theresa, to an fro. I want to join them. The long, black, shiny car comes down the road an tirns into our lane. It tirns round, heads back to the road an staps. The two men get out an waalk to the house. They wait by the front door. Mammy nods. More people line both sides of the lane an the road. Mammy takes me by the hand into the kitchen. My brothers an sister stand by the coffin. Mammy starts the rosary agen. When she's finished the two men lift the coffin lid standen against the wall, lay it flat on the coffin an tirn some screws. Granddad won't be able to get out. It'll be dark inside. He won't be able to move. Mammy's eyes are red. Daddy an Willie stand at wan end. The two men stand at the other. James an John stand in the middle. 'On the count of three, lift,' says wan a the men. 'One, two, three, lift.'

They balance the coffin on their shoulders wi' their arms round each other's neck. They shuffle back an forward to get the coffin through the door. They slide their feet along the cement path to feel the step down

At the end of Mass Father Kelly an the altar boys stand round the coffin. They kerry a small box with a spoon leanen on the edge an a round bowl hangen from a chain. Father Kelly takes a spoonful an drops the powder into the round bowl. He shuts the lid. He takes the chain from the altar boy. He lifts it over the coffin an moves it back an forth. Smoke comes from the metal bowl. I lake the smell. 'Mammy. Mammy, what's that for?'

'Shhh', pullen me closer.

The two men appear agen. They turn the coffin round an wheel it down. The altar boys an Father Kelly follow. The organ starts. Ivrybody stands an starts to sing. The women push their veils back to read the hymn. Some luck at me, some at Daddy and Mammy and some at the coffin. The men sing with deep voices. Some stay silent. I luck from side to side at the rows of faces. I luck longer at the wans I know but they don't say anythen. I don't know if I should speak or not. I luck at Mammy. I luck at the coffin. I luck at the floor of small wooden pieces. There's muck on me shoes. I jerk round. Mammy tightens her fingers round me wrist. She'll be cross because she polished them. I'll hev to clean them afore she sees them. The singen is louder near the middle of the aisle. I want the coffin to speed up. I poke me finger inside me collar.

The rain has stopped when we get outside. The trees round Father Kelly's house swish an bend with the strong breeze. Everyone tightens their coats, hats an scarves. Some crouch forward to keep balance. More people line the path. When the coffin is in the car it heads aff. We follow in Joe's car. I push meself up on the leather back seat to see out. I see McCarthy's Pub past the chapel. I luck from side to side but I don't know all the houses on the road. I think Uncle Danny and Auntie Sarah live here. 'Where are we, Mammy?'

'On our way to the graveyard.'

'Why?'

'To bury Granddad.' Mammy frowns. I keep quiet.

The black car groans as it climbs the steep hill to the graveyard at Lagg. We waalk behind it, pullen our coats tight an benden forward into the sea wind an rain. Sheep stand with their backs to it. The grass on the sand dunes bends. We stap at the big heap of clay. I shiver. Me ears sting. The men sit the coffin on two planks across a deep narrow hole. Two thick ropes lie underneath it. Four men pick up the ends of the ropes an raise the coffin. Their arms shake. They puff. Their feet shuffle an sink into the wet ground. Two others pull the planks away. The men feed the ropes through an lower the coffin. It sinks, sinks, sinks. It wobbles. It scrapes the sides of the hole. Bits of gravel faal. The lid disappears. The to the gravel. Mammy haulds me hand. We follow behind with Theresa, Cahir, Kevin an Dan.

Daddy an me other brothers shuffle along the gravel to the road. They stap at the back of the car. The men lower the coffin into the long boot wi' a high open door that seems to touch the sky. The coffin slides in on the shiny wooden floor. They shut the boot. 'Where's the car goen, Mammy? Ken I go? Where's Granddad goen?' I esk, tuggen her hand.

'Shhh, we're goen to the chapel for Mass,' pullen me back to the house to get into Joe Gorman's car. I luck back at the car headen aff. Will they let him out at the chapel? He might be asleep.

When we arrive at the chapel the car is waiten. Mammy haulds me hand. She leads me into the porch. People hunchen against the driven rain line both sides of the cement path. They nod, bow their heads an make the sign of the cross. The men take aff their caps an hauld them across their chest. They flatten their hair. The women hauld rosary beads an check their veils in the swirlen wind. Nobody speaks.

I peep round from behind Mammy. The two men wheel the coffin on the silver frame with four wheels into the porch. I luck at the altar. Father Kelly stares at us with his hands joined. An altar boy stands on either side of him. The wooden floor of the aisle shines. It makes them seem a long way away. He nods to the altar boys. They waalk to us. Father Kelly follows. His shoes clatter. His face is cross lake when he comes into school. I think of what Willie tauld me. I wonder if he hits the altar boys too. They luck scared. I tuck in beside Mammy. Nobody speaks. The organ starts. People shuffle to their feet. They cough an splutter. They start to sing but I ken't make out what they're sayen. The women on one side sing better than the men on the other. Mammy pulls me arm. 'Stop looking round. Face the front,' she whispers.

Father Kelly an the altar boys waalk up the aisle. He sings at the tap of his voice. It sounds lake he's shouten at ivrywan. The two men steer the coffin. Mammy, Daddy, my brothers an sister follow. I luck from side to side. Ivrywan seems tall. Their backs are broad. Their hats, caps, scarves an overcoats hide their faces. They're crowden over me. I look round. Father Kelly staps at the altar rail. He tirns round. The two men lave. Mammy an Daddy lead us into the two front empty rows. When the singen stops ivrybody sits down. Mass begins. I don't know all the Latin.

The red light flickers. It lucks lake a candle inside a red glass. Jesus ken't fit in there. He ken't get up there. He'll burn. I tug Mammy's arm an frown. I luck back at the light. There's a long chain hangen from the ceilen. He'll break the chain an faal. I frown at Mammy agen. Me neck hurts.

9

ropes go loose. They men pull the ropes out. Me teeth chatter. Me legs shake. Father Kelly sprinkles holy water into the hole. He grabs a handful of soil an draps it in. 'Mammy, he's throwen muck at Granddad.' Her eyes are red. She doesn't answer. 'How'll he get out, Mammy?'

'Come on, we're goen home now,' she whispers lucken back at the hole.

The door into Granddad's bedroom is half open. I peep in. He's not there. It feels cold. The fire's dead. His blue striped waistcoat and blue tie hang on the back of his chair. His white shirt collar an studs lie on the bed. His black rimmed glasses with wan arm stuck with Sellotape are on the table. His white potty sits under the metal bed.

I waalk past the sitten room. The door is open. I go in. The fire is dead. The curtains are shut. Chairs are against the wall. A smell fills the room. It must be the empty bottles of Guinness. The room is cold. Cards lie on the mantelpiece. I luck at Granddad's photo on the wall. There's another photo beside it. It's a lady. I don't know who she is.

Running Home

I sneak along the outside of the playground wall. I know I shouldn't be doen this. I don know why. It's playtime. The sun makes me sweat even afore I reach the end of the wall. The boys play near the toilet built against the wall. It stinks. There's a big hole in the middle of the long piece of wood. The bucket is underneath. Bits of newspaper hang on a rusty nail. There's some in the bucket, bits on the wood and some on the floor.

I run up the rodeen to the top of the hill. I think I can see our house. It's the only red roof. I don't know why it's called Crega. The rodeen down to the shore is steep an rough. This is the first time I've seen the fiels an river from up here. They look so wee. I wish I was a bird looken down on ivrythen. I try to work out which fiels are ours. They are steep. I must watch out for the loose gravel.

The water in the shuchs runs along the rodeen all the way down to the shore. It flows fast over stones. It disappears under the long grass an splashes into holes made by the cows an sheep. I slurp some water. Me teeth chatter. I splash some on me face. An auld bath is sunk in the shuch. Water splashes in one end an out the other. Green stuff floats on tap. Cow dung sticks on the edge.

I kerry on down the rodeen. The fiels an river seem bigger an flatter now. I sneak past the two houses at the end of the rodeen. The doors are open. A black dog sits near wan of them. I think it's Danny Shield's house. I hope the dog doesn't bark. I run. The river looks even bigger down here. The water is still an dark. Daddy said that means it's deep. I think this must be where he catches salmon. I want to go wi' him and see the big salmon fighten their way out of the net. 'You'll hev to wait a wee while longer. Yid faal in an be drownded,' he'd say.

'I'll be good. I promise.'

'I tauld ye afore. Yir not comen' th'day. Yid only act the maggot.'

Why he didn't fish duren th'day. He'd see better and I cuda gone too. I luck behind. The tap of the hill seems so far away. I ken't see the school. The cottages are smaller too. I luck for Crega. It seems so far away that I'll niver reach it. The house isn't below me anymore. I think I'm on the same level. There's smoke comen from the chimley. I kerry on down to the river jumpen over shuchs. I don't know what time it is. It must be after dinner. I'm scared.

I stand by the shuch I hev to cross. The barbed wire is too high to climb over. It's too loose to crawl through because the wooden posts hev been knocked down by the cows. The water is low. The sides are steep an slippery. I luck for the best place to cross. I find a spot where the wire is broken. I must watch out for the sinken sand. I balance wan foot on the first stone an the other foot on the bank. I move onto the middle stone. Just as I take the final step I slip on the slime. I pull me foot from me sinken shoe. I jump onto the bank. I grab the lace floaten on the water. I pull an pull until I get me shoe out. Me socks an trousers are wet an mucky. I bang me shoe on a stone. Some muck faals out. I take me sock aff an hobble up the slope. Me fut is freezen.

Crega lucks bigger. It seems so long since I left the school. I'm scared as I get nearer home. I'm too scared to return to school. I'll be in trouble with Mrs. Monaghan. I wonder what'll Daddy do to me. I thought the waalk wud be shorter. I button me coat. I'll niver do this agen. It seemed so easy to start with. I luck behind. It's too far to go back. The houses on the rodeen are white dots. Their windows an doors are smaller black dots. The rodeen up the hill is a thin brown wiggly line. Clouds cover the tap of it. I ken't believe I was up there. The smoke from our chimley is thicker. There are brown rain marks on the roof from the chimley down to the gutteren.

I slide under the wire fence near Gort na Mullen Bridge. I lean over. The water is still an brown. Bubbles pop up an burst. Daddy says it's a sign there are fish there. The dark stones make the water luck brown. On the other side the water ripples an flows fast. I throw in twigs an dash to the other side. They pick up speed. After a few tries I know where the next twig will pop up. I ken't understand what makes the twigs disappear an then appear agen. I lave the bridge an follow the road to our house.

I pass Roger Tamm's cottage. 'Roger, come here. Them damn sheep are in the tirnips agen.' I ken't see Rose but I know it's her shouten.

'Aaaaaaah, aaaaaaaaaah. I'll go now.'

Roger stumbles through the tirnips, throwen his arms in the air. The sheep kerry on munchen until he's within reach. He gives a loud grunt. They jump over the broken fence into the grass fiel. He leans back. He pants an pulls the wooden post with wire tied round it. The wire tears through the grass, bouncen an springen until it's in line with the rest of the fence. No matter how hard he tries he ken't push the post all the way into the hole. 'Get in ye fecken hoor ye.'

He wipes his face with his flat cap. The wire still sags on the grass. He stomps back to the house in his wellies, wan black an wan green. These must be the good wellies he keeps when he throws away the leaken ones. I want to know if they're two left wans, two right wans or wan of each. 'Ye ken't lave the wire lake that, ye amadan,' Rose bellows, leanen over the half door.

'Not fecken stupid. Where's the sledge?'

She slams the door. He storms round to the back of the house, kicken gravel. The chickens scatter.

I sneak up the brae along the hedge to Paddy and Biddy's house. Black smoke floats from the chimley. He's up a wooden ladder whitewashen the front of the house. His flat cap covers his ears an eyebrows. A bucket sits on the tap rung, tilted into the wall. 'Roof needs fecken thatchen agen. Them burds a hoor. Damn nests as well. Better aff wi' a fecken tile roof. More fecken money,' pointen his brush up to the thatch.

'Well, s'pose we save money in the long run. Ye'll hev to cut out the smoken an drinken,' replies Biddy in her squeaky laugh, standen at the foot of the ladder with her fists resten on her hips.

'No bloody chance. It's the only pleasure I hev,' a mouthful of tobacco splashen on her wellies.

'What ye fecken doen, ye dirty bugger.' She steps back an wipes it aff her wellie with a coat lyen on the footpath.

'Well, stay in the fecken house out a me way.'

The road to Micky Bulben's house is straight with barbed wire on both sides. There aren't any hedges until I get to the whin bushes at the corner. I luck behind. Nobody. Micky's door is closed. His dog is sleepen on the flagstones. His bicycle isn't by the front window.

I cut through the Rock's Fiel. Fairies live in the rocks. I luck between them but ken't see any. I climb to the tap an rest me back against wan. The sun warms me face. I feel safe here. No-one ken see me. I'm high up an ken see a long way. The sea is much further away. The waves crash against the rocks. The white foam shoots up, spreads out an slides down. The shuchs an rodeen have disappeared. The river wiggles its way round our fiels separaten us from The Merchant's, Kelly's, an Uncle Packie's farms. I want to play wi' cousin Patrick. Daddy won't let me.

I luck over me shoulder. The red roof scares me. I don't want to go any further. I want to stay. Daddy'll hit me. He'll take me back to school. Mrs. Monaghan will use the sally rod. I hope he's not in the house.

I lave The Rocks Fiel an crawl under the barbed wire into the fiel behind the house. Bits of sheep's wool rub me head. I sneak behind the diesel tank. It stands on two cement walls. Laddie an Shep lie at the back door. They stand up an wag their tails. They're too scared to bark after Daddy knocked it out of them wi' a stick. They come to me. I pat them on the head. I watch the door. I think it's about dinner time.

I ken't hear anywan apart from a voice on the radio. I want to run back to school. It'll take me too long to run back. I don't want to go into the scullery either. If Daddy's still eaten, his wellies should be standen by the door. Dishes rattle in the sink. Mammy must be washen up. Everybody must've eaten. No-one else must be inside. Water spurts down the gully. I freeze. I don't know what to do if she comes out. Two round wheaten scones rest on the inside of the window ledge with a cloth wrapped round them. The smell of the fresh bread makes me want to eat a warm, steamen, crusty slice with Mammy's butter an blackberry jam. The butter melten an the jam runnen over the edge. I lick me lips. The water staps. Mammy's shoes clatter along the linoleum. The noise fades. The liven room door squeaks. I luck back towards the barn. Nobody. I ken't stay here aal afternoon. Daddy'll catch me. I shuda thought of this afore.

The rumble of the Massey Ferguson makes me jump. I crawl to the side of the barn an crouch behind the potato digger. Daddy heads out of the barn. The tractor engine roars along the road puffen black smoke. His grey hair flutters backwards. He'll call to Aunty Mary Anne's shop for the things Mammy wants. Then he'll head to the school. I rub me eyes with the back of me hand. I stare at the open scullery door. I edge forward an rest me chin on the table where the churn stands. Its cold metal handle pokes me cheek. I jump. The dishes stand on the drainen board. A song starts on the radio. I think Mammy's in bed. The damp collar of me white shirt makes me shiver. Mammy'll go mad when she sees me socks, trousers an shoes. I take a glass of fresh water from the bucket. I gasp. I cover me mouth. The door squeaks. 'Oh, hello, Patrick. I didn't think you'd be home yet. I thought Daddy only went for you a few minutes ago.'

I luck at the floor. Mammy waalks past me. She turns on the gas cooker. 'Oh, God. This damned gas. It never lights without a fight.' She turns the gas aff an tries agen with another match. 'Thank God for that. I think we need a new bottle. Doesn't last long at all.'

The flames lick the bottom of the saucepan wi' the wooden handle that me brother John made. The smell of gas spreads. She starts to pull the churn handle until it's turnen at a steady speed. She asks me to help. I stand on a stool an grab the end of it. She lets go but I ken't turn it on me own. She holds me hand an we churn together. The blades inside thump, thump, thump. The milk splashes the sides. Mammy lifts the square lid.

'Not ready yet. Few more minutes should do it.'

'Can I luck?' Mammy haulds me arm as I step onto the table. Small yellow lumps stick to the blades. Some float on the milk an others slide down the side. The milk smells sour. She says that's normal. I hold me nose an step down. 'Another few turns and that'll do it, Patrick. The potatoes'll be about twenty minutes,' lucking at the clock. 'It's only three o'clock. Where's Daddy?'

She squints at me. I luck at her. I stare at the floor agen. She lets go of the handle. Steam begins to hiss from the saucepan. Mammy bangs the lid wi' her hand. I startle. The lid goes silent for a few seconds afore rattlen agen. 'How d'you get home?'

'Waalked.'

'What d'you mean? Walked?'

'Just waalked. I thought it was time to come home.'

'For God's sake, Patrick. You must've known it wasn't time. You'd have seen Daddy there.'

She stares at me wi' bulgen eyes before throwen the churn lid into the sink. I shake. I think of Daddy waiten at school. I luck at the clock. The big hand is at nine an the little hand is nearly at three.

Wi'out sayen a word, Mammy scoops out the big pieces of butter. She slides them onto a board. Wi' a butter pat in each hand she squeezes the lumps into a square. Yellow water dribbles onto the board. She laves the butter to drain aff afore wrappen it in paper. The butter pats land in the sink wi' such a thump they make me jump. She slams a metal jug down on the table. She tilts the churn to pour out the buttermilk. I step forward to help.

'Stay out of my way. You've done enough harm already.' I step backwards. I dry me eyes wi' me sleeve. She's niver tauld me to go away afore. I lake helpen Mammy. I hate to see her panten an screwen up her face. When the jug is full she pours the rest into a bucket for Daddy to feed the pigs. 'Look at your trousers. They're ruined. How am I supposed to get them clean for tomorrow? Look at your shoes.'

The Massey Ferguson races up the lane. The tyres screech on the gravel. Footsteps thump along the cement path. 'Jesus Christ, Lizzie.' Two boys follow him wi'out sayen a word. His shoulders touch the sides of the door frame. He lowers his head. The streaks of grey hair dangle from the side of his head an cover his left ear. He flattens them back on tap. 'Come here, ye little bugger. Where the hell hev ye ben?' He marches towards me with bulgen blue eyes, red cheeks an clenched fists.

'Don't,' shouts Mammy.

Tony an Philip from the tap class stand by the door an luck away. 'When I went into the shop Tony an Philip were esken about that little bugger. Mrs. Monaghan sent them out to luck for him,' as he moves nearer, pointen his white knuckles. 'How d'ye get here?'

I try to tell him.

'Hauld yir wisht. Ye cuda drownded. Wan slip an yid be a goner.'

'Go and change your clothes. I'll have to wash them quickly for tomorrow,' Mammy says.

'Come on, lads. Let's get ye home afore yir Mammy an Daddy start worryen. I'll see *ye* in a wee while,' glaren and pointen his finger.

I head down the corridor to me room an take aff me trousers. I sit on the bed. I dangle me legs over the side tryen to touch the carpet. I ken't decide whether to take me trousers to Mammy or not. I think I'll feel safer if I stay here. The belt on me trousers is thinner an shorter than Daddy's. It'll either be the belt or a couple of slaps round the head. The slaps make me dizzy an sick. Wi' the belt it's just a few stings on me bare backside. 'Patrick, your dinner's ready,' Mammy shouts from the end of the corridor.

My legs stap. I slip me trousers on. I waalk along the corridor. The smell of fish hits me. Oh, no, not herren agen. I'm not sure if the cooked smell is worse or better than the raw smell. If I didn't see Mammy choppen aff its head with its bulgen eyes, big mouth and cutten its silver stomach I might lake it better. I ken't stap thinken about its eyes. They watch me when I waalk through the kitchen. They're not supposed to move but I'm sure they do. I think of Mammy's staren eyes. They definitely move. Oh God, my stingen eyes. The herren eyes. Daddy's eyes.

The noise of the tractor engine gets louder as it passes the front of the house. It goes silent. I try to sneak out the door. 'Sit there and eat it.' Mammy dumps the saucepan an fryen pan in the sink. Heavy boots clatter on the path. I knock the chair over. I dash towards the door. 'Get back here and sit down.'

Daddy appears at the backdoor. He stares. He waalks out. I wipe the tears with me sleeve an force a forkful down. I'm goen to be sick. He'll come back when Mammy's not here. He'll wait as long as he has to. I know he'll get me afore he goes to bed.

Mammy rushes me to the bathroom. She washes me face an tucks me up in bed. She shuts the door an tiptoes along the corridor. I know she's angry but when I've been in trouble afore she was alright the next day. I shiver. I cry. I pull the sheets over me head. Daddy's footsteps clump along the path outside me window on his way to the kitchen. Mammy's voice is louder than his. I ken't make out what she's sayen.

He'll sit. He'll stare at the floor. He'll rest wan elbow on the table. He'll listen. He'll say nothen. He knows better than to argue wi' her. When he gets me later he'll threaten me not to tell her.

Ivrywhere is quiet. Mammy must've done the washen up and is resten in the liven room. Daddy must be heven his boiled egg, bread, butter an tea in the kitchen. The sun goes behind the hedge. It's getten colder. The liven room door squeaks. I hope it's Mammy. 'Daddy wants you,' she says, openen me door'.

I follow her to the kitchen. Daddy's standen with the slipper in his fist. 'Get here now,' grabben me round me neck. He pulls me to his chair. He sits down. He pushes me neck down. Me stomach flops onto his knees. I try to raise me head but he pushes all the harder. My legs dangle. He pulls me pyjamas down. I try to luck round. His hand is in the air. I wait. 'This'll teach ye. Don't ye iver do a stupid thing lake that agen.' I scream.

When he has finished he pushes me away. 'Get to bed an stay there,' he shouts. His blue eyes bulge. I pull up me pyjamas. The waist elastic stings. The slipper bounces aff the door as I open it. I duck and run.

Brendan

I stand on the wooden chair an gawk out of the kitchen window at Joe Gorman's car pullen up at the front door. Mammy's sitten in the back seat. I ken't see her face behind a white bundle. He opens the door. He takes the bundle. Mammy slides out an takes the bundle from Joe. He grabs the brown suitcase. It used to be on the bottom shelf on the press. They chat in the hallway. I ken't make out what they're sayen. The kitchen door opens. She smiles. 'Come in Joe. This is Brendan, Patrick.'

'Right, Lizzie. There y'are.'

He puts the case on the floor near the table. He shuts the door. He shuts the front door. He shuts the boot.

'Oh. Run quick with this.' I grab the money an dash out.

'Mammy's tauld me to give ye this.'

'Get away wi' ye,' shutten the car.

I watch him drive away. I luck in the barn for Daddy. I want to tell him Mammy's come home with baby Brendan. He's not there. A cow moos. It must be calven because there's a bottle of Dettol an a bucket of water near the byre door. I know he won't let me in. I go back inside. I want to see Brendan. Mammy's resten her head on the back of the chair. 'Thanks, Patrick,' she whispers.

She shuts her eyes. I sit on Daddy's chair at the far end of the kitchen. I stare at her. I want to esk Mammy where Brendan's come from, but I don't know what to say. I kept esken Daddy when Mammy was comen home but he wudn't tell me. I have a little brother. That makes me an older brother. I'm bigger an stronger. I'm not a baby anymore. I step forward. The blanket moves. A fist the size of a hen egg appears. A gurgle. A bald head moves sideways. The blanket slides down. His fist rubs his face. Another gurgle. He starts to scream. His face goes red. His fists clench. A shriek. I dash back to the chair. 'Oh, Jesus, Mary and Joseph. I was sound asleep.' Mammy screws up her face. She slides aff the chair. She groans. She puts Brendan on the table. 'He'll need a clean nappy.'

A nappy? She opens the blanket an his white gown. His arms an legs luck lake the wans on the brown teddy by his head. She lifts his legs wi' wan hand an removes a white cloth from his backside. I ken use the toilet. I don't understand why she ken't take him to the toilet. 'Get me the white bucket under the sink in the scullery.' I run. I reach in an take it out. It's plastic. A white cloth lies in the bottom. I empty it out. I pick up the bucket by the white handle. The bottom is yellow an scraped. A thin brown line goes all the way round the inside about halfway up. I wonder if Mammy used it for me when I was a baby. When I return, the nappy's rolled up on the floor. A yellow stain seeps through. It lucks the same colour as a newly born calf when it shits. I turn away. I hauld me nose. Mammy shakes white power on Brendan's backside. She puts another nappy on. I stare at the big pin goen through the cloth. She'll stab him. The end appears. She snaps the pin shut. The yellow stain gets bigger. Mammy puts the cloth in the bucket. 'Put it near the back door. I'll soak it.'

I hold me nose again an stretch my arm out as I kerry it to the kitchen. I put it by the door without lucken at it. I feel sick. 'Would you like to touch Brendan?' I shake me head. I step back. 'Well, get the pram from the sitten room. I just don't have the energy.'

I'm not allowed in. That's where Granddad died. That's me pram. He's not goen to die in me pram. I shake my head. 'Just go and get the pram,' raisen her voice.

I don't want Brendan here. Please take him away. I don't want a younger brother. I want to run outside. The cow staps mooen. She must've calved. Daddy always shuts the byre door when a cow's calven. The byre door squeaks. Daddy comes out wi' his sleeves rolled up past his elbows. He washes his hands in the bucket of Dettol. It's the same smell as when the vet comes. I can smell it when Daddy has his dinner. He walks past the window.

I open the sitten room door. The last time I was in here was for granddad's corphouse. The same row of chairs hides me pram behind the door. It's still covered with a green bedsheet. I rub the blue cloth hood. It's folded flat. I rub the silver tubes above the wheels. The wheels have silver spokes an white rubber tyres. There are black marks on them. The front wheels come up to me knee. The back wans reach me waist. I raise meself up on me toes to luck inside. I rub the mattress. The white sheet is soft lake sheep's wool. I want to climb in an rest me face on it. I rub the white blanket against me cheeks. Camphor. The same smell as in the drawers an wardrobe in me bedroom, on Mammy's cardigan, an Daddy's suit. 'What's taking you so long?'

'Comen.'

I throw the blanket back. The silver handle shines through the worn rubber. Me nose touches it. It smells lake the smoke from the tractor tyres when they spin on gravel. I push the pram near Mammy. Bits of rubber stick to me hands. She rests Brendan on his back an covers him wi' the white blanket. He makes fists. They lie by his ears. Mammy flops back into the armchair. She drops her head back an sighs. I stroke the blanket near Brendan's feet, then his tummy, then his chest. I move closer to his head. 'Can you rock him a bit?' Mammy raises her head when I don't answer. 'Just hold the handle and move it up and down a little.'

I rub the bits of rubber off me hands. The pram rocks lake me toy boat in the cows' drinking trough. 'That's it. He'll be asleep in no time.'

Anne Kelly from Killourt calls in. 'Hello Lizzie. It's good to see ye home agen. Congratulations! He's a fine lucken wee fella. Sure, he's the spittin' image a his Daddy an Dan.'

'You can't mistake our red hair. We're not called Jimmy Roe for nothing.'

'He's healthy. That's the main thing.' Mammy picks up Brendan an hands him to Anne.

'Here, hold him and I'll put the kettle on.'

'No, ye won't. Ye just sit down and I'll make the tae.'

'Ah, hold your tongue and take him.' Anne smiles at him. He gurgles. I sit by the window rubben me hands. I wonder where Daddy is. It's odd with a baby in the house. He's me little brother. I'll have someone to play with. The cups rattle. The kettle hisses.

'You'd be better off getting some fresh air. Run outside and see what they're doing.' I don't want to go outside. I want to listen to Mammy an Anne. I lake it when people come. Auntie Rose an Uncle Danny from Derry bring sweets an cakes when they come. Daddy chats to them. They laugh. I wish Daddy would come in an see Brendan. I don't want Daddy to stay in the house. I lake it when it's just her an me. She taalks more to me. Mammy kerries the tray of cups an the teapot. I kerry the jug a milk an go back for the plate a fig rolls an digestive biscuits. I take wan a each an sit down.

'You know, Anne, he'll be out there on the farm before you know it, getting covered in muck and jumping on tractors like his brothers.'

'How did it go anyway?'

'Go outside and play, I said.' When Mammy lucks at me with that face I know it's time to move. I shuffle to the kitchen an open the back door. I stand at the door an listen.

'Well, I'm still very sore. I've got some stitches.'

'What d'ye mean? Stitches?'

'He's a big baby. Eleven pounds six ounces. He's the biggest of them all.' 'Jesus, Mary and Joseph. What a weight.'

'Well, I ended up ripping. He just wouldn't come out. God, the pain. He'll be the last I'm telling you. God, eight boys and one girl.'

'God bless us an save us, Lizzie, that's tarrible. I ken't imagine the pain.'

'The doctor says the stitches'll come out soon.'

Mammy went to hospital. She came home with Brendan. They must be talken about the cow calven. Daddy still has two cows waiten to calf. They must be talken about them. He used to taalk about a rope but Mammy hasn't mentioned a rope. Mammy hasn't been to the doctor. Maybe she means the vet. Brendan begins to cry. 'I'll take him. I think he'll want a feed.'

I run out to the sandpit at the barn gable. I hope Brendan can play with me soon. The trucks I made from pieces of wood, jam jar lids an empty shoe polish tins are wet. The nails are rusty. I shouldn't use the nails an tools from the barn. If I esk Daddy he won't let me. It's hard to hammer a nail into the wood. I cry when I bang me finger. I don't tell anywan. The nail bends. The wood splits an the wheel wobbles. I don't use jam jar lids anymore because they're too thin. They sink into the sand. The shoe polish tins are thicker. They move better because I put the nail all the way through. My trucks are lake real trucks with thick black tyres. I build roads with straight parts an dangerous bends. I dig tunnels in the sand. Sometimes a wheel faals aff. The trailer sinks because it's kerryen too much slat mara from the shore or too many cows for the market. The tunnel collapses. I brrrrrm brrrrrm so much that spittle wets me chin an dribbles onto me shirt. The sand rubs into me trousers. Mammy won't be happy. She'll hev to wash them afore I go to school. Sand creeps into me socks. I try to clear it out but there's always some left. Even after Mammy washes them wi' Daz I can still feel it.

Santa brought me a toolbox wi' a hammer, a saw, a screwdriver an a ruler. They have their own special places to slot into. I clean them afore shutten the box an take it indoors. The leather handle is soft. I'm a proper carpenter now. When John came home from America, he made me a pair of pliers. I'd lake to be a carpenter lake him. I wish I cud make things lake him. I bet he niver bangs his fingers. I would lake to go to America, build houses an learn how to make pliers. I don't lake it here.

When I see Anne laven I go back into the house. Brendan lies in his pram in the corner. I peep over the edge. He's still. He's quiet. Mammy squints at me from the settee. She feeds him wi' a bottle. She puts him over her shoulder an rubs his back. He burps. She changes his nappy.

The bucket is nearly full ivry day. The washen line at the end a the house sags wi' the flappen nappies. Daddy bends to avoid them. He comes in. He eats. He glances at the pram. He doesn't speak. He goes out. He takes me to school. I can't wait to get home. I want to esk Daddy about Brendan. When I come home I peep into his pram. His blue eyes are wider. I think he smiles. I smile. He flaps his arms an kicks his legs.

I rub his hand. He grips me finger. He pulls it to his mouth. 'It's a nice evening. We should take Brendan down to the shore,' Mammy says.

I push the pram. Its handle is near me nose. The sun glares in our faces. Daddy drives the cows into the byre for milken. He doesn't luck at us. We waalk past Paddy's, Biddy's an Roger's houses. Me arms get tired. Mammy pushes. We cross the bridge near the shore. I luck for the rodeen up the hill where I waalked home from school. I ken't see it.

Afore bedtime Mammy haulds Brendan on wan arm over the same sink she baths me in. She dribbles water over his tummy an legs. She wipes his head an face with a cloth. He frowns an rubs his fists over his cheeks. He doesn't cry. She mustn't be usen the same soap she uses on me. Mammy dries him an sprinkles white powder over him. She dresses him an places him in the pram. He gurgles. Her eyes luck redder without her glasses. Her hair lies flat. It lucks greasy.

Driving to Carnryan

I packed my green holdall, hung my black suit from a handgrip in the car. I laid the AA Road Atlas on the passenger seat. I filled my flask and headed north from Morecambe at three in the morning. I drove along the M6 and A75 through Lancashire, Cumbria, Drumfires, Galloway and Ayreshire for the eight o'clock Carnryan – Larne ferry.

The telephone had rung on Friday evening. It was the 25th September, 1992. I answered as Sheila stood listening in the kitchen, her grey coat still on. She handed me a tissue while stretching out her arms to hug me. We comforted each other with speechless sobs.

'The ice cream. Need to put it in the freezer,'

'Forget the ice-cream. I'll sort it.'

We emptied the shopping bags without being aware of what we were doing. In a shaking voice, I volunteered the details.

'Patrick?'

'Yes.'

'I'm afraid I've got bad news for you.' A silence fell. I waited for my sister Theresa to continue. 'Daddy died this morning.'

'Oh Jesus.'

'He had a heart attack in the car outside Malin Town.'

It was Monday. He'd have been driving home from the market in Carndonagh. Mammy would've been with him. 'Mammy's ok.'

From time to time the lights from an isolated car or lorry flashed through the central reservation as they came into view over the brows and wide bends of the M6. Some dimmed their lights. Some didn't. The tyres hummed and clattered over the joints between the tarmac sections. Nobody exited from the motorway services. I slowed down at the A75 junction. Specks of light in the distance indicated the waking farmers.

Warning signs of dangerous bends and accident spots urged me to concentrate on the stretch ahead. I sipped the last of the coffee. I followed the Carnryan sign. A crimson dawn rose through the cloud. The Stena Ferry sign showed above a hedge. My shoulders relaxed. I smelled the salty air and the oily stink of freight lorries. A string of halogen lights danced on the water amid the jetsam. Two red crosses shone above the security barrier. I turned off the engine. Seagulls squawked.

Sacraments

Ivry time I go into the barn they're lyen on the windowsill. Their blunt teeth stick up from the old nuts, bolts, wrenches an squeezers for crushen bull-calf testicles. The silver paint on the handles of the clippers is cracked. I want to hide them or break them, maybe bend a couple of teeth, jam clay between them or loosen a screw.

'Sit on the chair,' Daddy orders.

He stands behind me. He doesn't speak. I stare at the horse's collar hangen from a metal peg in the wall with a pair of hames strapped round its black leather. A hay rake dangles from a nail in the rafters. A tirf spade with a sheep's horn handle hangs from a rope. Laddie, the sheepdog, comes in wi' her tail between her legs. She settles on a bale of straw. Daddy throws a towel with loose threads an rat holes round me shoulders. He pushes me head forward with wan hand an pulls me collar back wi' the other. He pushes the hard edge of the towel down to me shoulders. I hauld me nose. He squeezes the handles of the clippers together. They squeak. He squirts three-in-wan oil along the spring an rubs it on his dungarees. The cold metal presses into me neck. I wait for the teeth to nip. He clicks, clicks, clicks worken his way up round me ears. The breeze chills me neck. He presses hard. Bits faal inside me collar. He pushes his left hand on tap of me head an bends it right, left, forwards an backwards. His fingers dig in. His right hand presses the handles. Clumps stick in the teeth. He pulls. I twitch. I freeze. I screw up me face. I slide me hand out from under the towel an wipe me eye. I push out me lower lip an blow the hair fallen over me eyes an nose. Me ears itch. I want to rub them. Daddy moves to me left, crouchen over me head. He bends me ear flat. He digs the teeth into me skull to make a neat edge. He steps to the right. He does the same again. Me skin stings. He stands in front of me. I stare at the silver buckles on his dungarees. He slides the sharp edge of the teeth along me forehead. It stings. He stands behind me. He yanks the towel from me neck. 'Right, there ye are.'

I stand up an look at the pile of hair on the floor. Me head is cold. I bend forward an rub me head. Some hair faals. Me hair feels firm an spikey. I rub me collar. I rub me neck. Me back itches. I walk along the path to the front door. Me head is colder. I rub me forehead. A speck of blood appears on me finger. I feel as bald as the last time. They'll laugh at me tomorrow. I wish Mammy would cut me hair. I head to the mirror. Me ears stick out. Me hair stands up. I pull it. I spit on me hand to flatten it. It doesn't move. I pull aff me shirt an waft it round. Me skin itches less when I put it back on. I cry. I wonder who cuts his hair. He just comes home with a fresh haircut. I'd lake to cut it. I wudn't use a towel. I'd dig the clippers into his neck an yank them when they stuck. I'd cut only wan side of his head lake he did to Johnnie Den across the river as a joke.

When I wake up in the mornen me head still feels cold. I check in the mirror. Me hair feels short. I pull it. Me ears luck bigger. Me neck seems longer. Mammy comes in. 'Get your best clothes on for the chapel. Mrs. Monaghan said you have to be there for a quarter past nine for your practice.'

I rehearse me list of sins that Mrs. Monaghan made us make up. 'Bless me, Father, for I hev sinned. It's a week since me last confession. I've had bad thoughts. I've stolen sweets from Aunty Mary Anne's Shop. I've cursed an I forgot to say me prayers before going to bed.'

I whisper the *Act of Contrition*. 'O my God, I am sorry for me sins because I hev offended ye. I know I should love ye above all things. Help me to do me penance, to do better, an to avoid anythen that might lead me to sin. Amen.'

We waalk the half mile to The Star of The Sea Catholic Church. Mrs. Monaghan stands at the door. 'Good morning, Mrs. Doherty. A big day today.' I luck down the aisle. Children from me class sit in two benches at the front. They luck round at me. Some of them cover their mouths an snigger.

'Go and sit with the others, Patrick. I'll be with you in a minute.' I tiptoe up the aisle an sidle into the seat. Mrs. Monaghan follows. Her shoes shuffle along the shinen wooden floor. She stands in front of us, crosses her arms an stares. 'I hope you remember what to say when you go into the confessional box. Father Kelly will want you to practise everything properly.'

A door at the side of the altar creaks. Father Kelly comes in. His black shiny shoes clatter. His black soutane swishes round his feet as he heads to the altar. A long, thin, white scarf sways over his stomach. He genuflects on the cement step, bows his head an blesses himself. We watch in silence. Black patches on his sole show where the brown leather has worn through. 'Good morning, Mrs. Monaghan.'

'Good morning, Father Kelly,' smilen at him.

'Shall we get started?'

'Yes, Father,' nodden at him.

'Right, children, I'm going into the confessional box over there to get ready. Mrs. Monaghan will send you to me one by one. While a child is with me the next one waits on the seat near the confessional box. You come in when the other child comes out. When you come out you go and kneel on the far side of the altar and say your penance. Is that clear?'

'Yes, Father Kelly,' we reply.

Father Kelly clatters down the side of the chapel. He shuts the confessional box door behind him.

'Right, Josephine, off you go. Knock on the door before you enter. Patrick, you sit on the end of the bench and be ready to go in when Josephine comes out.'

'Yes, Mrs. Monaghan.'

I stare at the door. I luck at the others on the front row. Some luck round. Others luck towards the altar. I whisper me list of sins agen and agen. The door opens. Josephine stares at the floor. She heads to the altar. Mrs. Monaghan nods to me to go in. A strip of wood covered in black leather rests on the floor to kneel on. A small metal grill is at head height. Brown wood covers the walls to the ceilen. I shut the door. Daylight shines in at the bottom of the door. I kneel. I wait. Silence. I luck upwards. I ken't see. I luck behind. I ken't see. He coughs. He shuffles. He slides the square grill. 'In the name of the Father and The Son and The Holy Ghost.' My hands shake. 'Bless you, my child. What is your confession?'

'Bless me, Father, for I hev sinned. It's a week since me last confession. I've had bad thoughts. I've stolen sweets from Aunty Mary Anne's Shop. I've cursed an forgot to say me prayers before goen to bed.'

'Is there anything else?'

'No, Father.'

'For your penance, say three Hail Marys.'

'Yes, Father Kelly.'

'Now say the Act of Contrition. O my God, I am sorry for…'

He stops. I continue. 'O my God, I am sorry for me sins because I hev offended ye. I know I shud love ye above aal things. Help me to do me penance, to do better, and to avoid anythen that might lead me to sin. Amen.'

'You did very well, my child. You can go now.'

'Thank ye, Father.'

'Tell the next child to come in.'

'Yes, Father Kelly.'

I grope for the knob. I nod to Angela to go in. I kneel at the far side of the altar. He didn't shout at me. He spoke in a quiet voice. It'll be ok this afternoon when I hev the proper First Confession. I'll get me certificate. Mammy'll be pleased. 'Hail Mary, full of grace, the Lord is with thee…' I say the three Hail Marys. I luck towards Mrs. Monaghan. She nods. I genuflect an head to the back of the chapel.

'Well, how was that?' Mammy asks.

'I did ivrythen right. I thought he'd shout but he didn't.'

'You remembered your sins?'
'Yes.'
'Well done. You'll need them for this afternoon. You'll need a good scrub'.

A week after it's First Holy Communion. My soul is clean now after confession. I mustn't sin afore Corpus Christi. Mammy stands me in the lukewarm water an hands me the pink bar of carbolic soap. 'Sit in there. Wash your neck and behind your ears. I'll come back and wash your hair. Use the scrubbing brush to clean your nails. Father Kelly'll be looking at them.'

When she comes back she squirts shampoo on me head. She rubs an rubs. The foam runs down me forehead. It doesn't sting lake the soap she used to use when I sat on the kitchen sink. 'Close your eyes,' splashen water over me head from a plastic jug. 'Let me see those nails. Right, out you get,' handen me a large blue towel.

I shiver. Me teeth chatter. Me head aches. I rub the towel all over me body. I follow Mammy to me bedroom. 'Here's your new clothes. Get dressed quickly. I'll do your tie.' I put on the white shirt. The collar is stiff. The button won't go through the hole. I pull on the grey trousers. The crease at the front runs in a straight line all the way down. It bends over me feet. I push the metal prong of the belt buckle hard. 'Are you nearly ready?'

I grab me red tie, me black coat an First Holy Communion badge. I run to her. The back door is open. Water splashes in the sink. Daddy washes an shaves. 'Give me your tie,' pullen up my collar. She ties the knot, forces the button through the hole an slides the knot up to me neck. I swallow. I move me neck from side to side. She haulds out the coat. I push me arms through. 'Turn round while I pin the badge on your lapel. Right, get your shoes on. You'll have to make sure you don't scrape them. You need some Brylcreem on that hair of yours.' She rubs a dollop between her palms an ruffles me hair. She combs it. She flicks a piece of fluff from the shoulder of me black jacket. Daddy waalks past me, his cheeks shinen. His thick vest hangs over his trousers. 'Wait here,' as she goes into their bedroom an shuts the door.

I luck out the window. The whin bushes down the lane bend in the breeze. Two cars arrive on the chapel carpark. I wonder who they are. I wish we had a car. I wriggle me toes. The shoes hurt the tap of me feet. I stand up. I waalk up an down the kitchen. They loosen a little.

Mammy comes out wearen her matchen green an brown tap an skirt. Her brown laced shoes make her luck taller. She checks her hair in the mirror on the sideboard. She pats round her ears. Daddy appears wearen his tweed hat tilted to wan side. A thin blue an green feather sticks out from the grey band. He pokes his finger behind the button of his white collar an pulls. He lucks in the mirror an pushes the knot of his blue tie back in place. He stretches his neck back. 'This damned collar's too tight,' he grumbles glancen at Mammy. She doesn't reply. He lucks at his shinen black shoes. He shakes his blue trouser leg to make the end cover his laces. He pats the tie on his stomach before buttonen his blue jacket. He heads out the front door an stands on the step lucken back to see where Mummy an I are. He only goes out the front door when he's dressed up to go somewhere. I don't understand.

'Come on, we better get going or your father'll head off without us,' Mammy says, nudging me. He heads down the lane. We follow. We quicken our step. We waalk past Mary Anne's Shop. He waves to her as she locks her door. She waves back. Mammy slows down to wait for her but speeds up agen when she sees Daddy moven further away. My left shoe rubs me heel. I wriggle me toes. I pull me sock up.

When we arrive at the chapel door, Mrs. Monaghan is standen with her arms folded. She stares. 'Good Morning, Mr and Mrs Doherty.'

'Good morning, Mrs. Monaghan,' Mammy replies while Daddy nods.

'Patrick, you go straight up to the front seat on the righthand side and kneel with the other boys.' I walk down the aisle. I luck round. Mammy an Daddy follow me halfway down. They genuflect an move into a bench. People sit squashed in benches on both sides. I kerry on up to the altar. I luck left. The girls from me class, in white dresses an white veils, kneel on the front bench. Their hands, in white laced gloves, join together pointen under their chin. The girls don't move. I luck right. The boys in black jackets, grey trousers, white shirts, red tie an red badge, kneel facen the altar. Their hair is flat an shines with Brylcreem. They join their hands pointen under their chin. I genuflect. I slide into the bench. I stare at the altar rail with the white cloth stretched all the way along the tap. The brown leather kneelen pad shines. I think of what Mrs. Monaghan kept shouten at us in school. 'Close your eyes. Put your tongue out properly. Make sure it's clean. Don't let it stick to the roof of your mouth. It's the body of Christ. It's a mortal sin. You'll have to go to Confession immediately.'

I luck sideways. The boys stare at the altar. I luck straight ahead again. Me *Before Communion Prayer*. I must say it or it'll be a sin. I make the sign of the cross. 'Lord Jesus, come to me, Lord Jesus, give me yer love. Lord Jesus, friend of children, come to me. Lord Jesus, ye are me Lord an me God. Praise to ye, Lord Jesus Christ.'

When it comes to Communion time Mrs. Monaghan stands at the end of the girls' bench. She nods. They stand. They line up wan behind each other with hands still pointen under their chin. Mrs. Monaghan nods agen. Maureen leads to the end of the altar rail. They kneel. They slide their hands under the white cloth. Father Kelly moves along the rail, holds up the host an places it on their tongue. Mrs. Monaghan nods to the boys. We line up an kneel on the altar rail. I slide me hands under the white cloth. I luck sideways. Father Kelly approaches. With the silver chalice in his left hand, he picks out a circular white host with his right hand an shows it to each of us. 'Corpus Christi,' he repeats to each boy.

'Amen'. It must be Latin. Mrs. Monaghan niver told us what it means.

Father Kelly moves in front of me. He haulds up the host an lucks at me. It's whiter an smaller than the circles of paper we practised wi' in school. The altar boy slides a silver plate under me chin. 'Corpus Christi,'
'Amen.'

I put me head back. I shut me eyes. I put me tongue out. I wait for the host. It rests on me tongue. It's dry. It sticks to me tongue. I close me mouth. I get up. I wobble because I'm not allowed to take me hands away from me chin. I sidle into me seat. I wobble agen. I kneel.

The hosts goes soggy. I want to suck it. I ken't. It'll be a mortal sin. I swallow. Some of it's gone. I'll hev to go to Confession. Father Kelly'll shout at me. He'll tell Mrs. Monaghan. She'll shout too. She'll tell Mammy. Mammy'll be upset. Me prayer. Me *After Communion Prayer.*

'Lord Jesus, I love an adore ye. Ye're a special friend to me. Welcome, Lord Jesus. Thank ye for comen to me. Thank ye, Lord Jesus, for given yerself to me. Make me strong to show yer love wheriver I may be.' I swallow. I move me tongue. The host's gone. I don't hev to tell anywan. I look sideways. I smile. The boys smile back.

'Could the boys and girls come up and stand at the altar rail in the same order,' Father Kelly announces at the end of Mass. He stands an watches us. He's goen to tell us aff. He knows I've swallowed the host. He'll tell ivrybody.

'Congratulations to all the children for making their First Holy Communion today. I'm now going to present them with their certificates which I hope they will put on display at home to show everyone that Jesus lives in them.'

He moves along the rail, takes the certificates from the altar boy an hands them to us. 'Congratulations, Patrick,' shaken my hand. I hold the cream card. A picture of The Last Supper is on the top half. Underneath in thick black handwriting it says:

Patrick Martin Doherty
Received
The Sacrament of Holy Communion
At
The Star of The Sea Catholic Church
On
Thursday 28th May 1959

Celebrant: Father Kelly

What is 'celebrant?' I niver heard the word afore. 'I want you all to face the congregation now. When the organ starts Mrs. Monaghan will lead you down the aisle. Hold your certificates in front of you for everyone to see them.'

The 15th

It's Sunday. The grinden noise wakes me. I open me eyes. It stops. I sit up an luck at the clock. It's half past seven. Somethen bangs outside. It sounds lake a hammer hitten wood. I slide the curtain open. The barn door is open. Planks of wood lie on the gravel. A saw rests on a barrel. It must be me brother, John. He said he was goen to make the frame for the 'throwen the sheaf' competition at Sports Day the morra. He lifts wan end af a long plank lyen on the trailer. He pulls it until the other end rests on the edge of the trailer. He raises it above his head an lowers it onto his shoulder. He slides it along until it balances. He steadies his feet an gets ready to lift. He moves his hands along an heaves himself up. He puffs. A hammer an pliers dangle from his leather tool belt. They sway.

    I pull on me jeans, checked shirt an blue jumper. I dash out the front door. The sound of Daddy's whistle makes me luck towards The Homes Fiel on the other side of the midden. The six sheep he bought from Bobby Henderson, up the road, scatter everywhere. I don't understand why he buys sheep from Bobby. He's a Protestant.

    'Come by,' he shouts at Shep.

    Shep runs. The sheep scatter.

    'Way,' Daddy calls, hitten his long stick on the grass. Shep runs the other way. The sheep gather together by the midden wall.

    'Sit.' Shep cowers in the grass.

    I kerry on to the barn. 'Mornen,' John smiles.

    'Ken a help ye?' I ask.

    'Aye. Get me that tape measure from the binch. A need two planks fifteen fut long for the uprights.' I hauld wan end. He slides the tape measure along the plank resten on the barrel. He takes the thick pencil from behind his ear. He wets it between his lips an marks the wood. 'Pass me the saw, will ye an then hauld the far end.' I grip it wi' both hands an lean over. John lays the saw teeth along the pencil line an drags it backwards wi' his right hand. His left thumb rests against the flat metal to keep it in place. A thin line of fresh wood appears. He drags backwards agen afore pushen an pullen the saw deeper an deeper. Saw dust bounces along an makes a heap on the concrete floor. 'Put yer hands underneath now to stap it faalen aff.'

    We kerry the plank outside an lay it alongside the other wan. We lift two thinner planks out a the trailer an cut them for the crossbars. 'Why do ye need two crossbars?'

'Ye need wan across the middle to hauld the uprights in place an then ye need the other wan to slide up an down for people to throw the sheaf over.'

'How'll ye move it up an down?'

'Wi' a rope. Ye'll see when it's finished.' John drills holes at the ends of the first crossbar an in the middle of the uprights for the bolts. 'Ken ye get me two bolts from the box on the trailer? We'll need 'em at the sports fiel tonight.'

'Ken a come along wi' ye?'

'Ye may as well. A cud do wi' a han to hauld the uprights.' John stretches the tape measure along the tap half a the uprights an makes a mark ivry futt. He drills holes on each mark. He screws in a metal hook at the tap of the planks.

'What's the hook an all them holes for?'

'I'll tie a rope to the second crossbar an feed it through the hook. When somebody throws the sheaf over the crossbar wi' a fork, I'll pull the rope an the bar'll go up wan notch. Then I'll stick a peg in wan of the holes.'

'A don't understand.'

'Tell ye what. I'll show ye this evenen. Ye ken even hev a go yerself.'

'Is the sheaf heavy?'

'Heavy enough. It cud break the fork if ye're weren't careful.'

Mammy appears at the barn door. She stares. John staps. 'I've been looking for you, Patrick. It's half past eight. We're going to Mass in an hour. For God's sake, John, could you not have waited until after Mass? What's Father Kelly going to say if he finds out?' John lucks at the floor. He lucks at me. We follow Mammy into the kitchen. 'You need to get yourselves washed and changed. We'll have to set off in half an hour or we'll be late.'

We all head aff at half past nine. The drizzle has stapped. The clouds over The White Strand are moven out to sea. When we arrive at the door of the chapel Father Kelly is standen there. He has a sheet in his hand. He writes on it as he talks to people enteren. He'll be checken who's comen to the sports. He'll ask the men what they've done to get the fiel ready. He'll read out their names on the altar, lake he does when they don't bring tirf for his fire in the winter.

'Good morning, everyone,' Father Kelly says as he moves into the middle of the doorway. 'You're still taking part in the sheep dog trials tomorrow, aren't you, Willie?' turnen to Daddy.

'Aye, I'll be there, Father.'

'We'll have to beat the Derry men. They say their dogs don't understand our sheep.'

'All the better for me, then,' Daddy smiles.

'I'll be making sure you run in the races, Patrick.' I luck at him. I don't want to run. I'll hide in the crowd. Ivrybody'll be lucken at me. Mr. Quigley'll shout at me on the fiel. He'll be drunk.

'And John, you're doing Throwing the Sheaf if I'm right.'

'Aye, I am, Father. I'll be putten it up this evenen.'

'And you'll be doing the teas, Lizzie?' She lucks at him. She smiles. She doesn't speak. Mammy doesn't go the Sports Day. She stays at home by herself.

Father Kelly writes notes on his sheet. The ends of his wide white sleeves flap in the breeze. He flattens his grey strands of hair danglen over his ears. We go inside. After the gospel readen, he closes The Bible. He opens his sheet of paper. He flattens it on the altar. We sit an wait. He lucks at it. He lowers his glasses onto the end of his nose an stares at us. He lucks right an left. He splutters. He reads out the names of the men who hevn't helped to prepare the fiel. People cough. They shuffle. Footsteps make me luck round. Mickey Bulben waalks to the back an laves. 'That Father Kelly has a lot to answer for. It's no wonder he can't get people to help,' Mammy says on the way home.

After breakfast, John an I go to the barn to finish aff the frame. He checks the holes on both uprights to make sure they match up. He lucks round for auld six-inch nails an straightens em on the anvil with a hammer. 'Throw 'em in that bucket. There shud be some vice grips on the binch. Don't forget the spirit level. Ken ye get some posts from the shed. We need eight for supports.'

I go to the back of the barn an kerry wan in each han every time. John sharpens the ends with a hatchet. We load ivrythen onto the trailer an head to the fiel behind Barney Grant's Pub. Wet bunten, hangen from whin bushes an barbed wire along the road, flap in the strong breeze.

'It better be drier the morra or there'll be no sports at all,' John shouts over the roar of the tractor engine. I nod. He drives the tractor through the gate, over the shore gravel coveren the mud. The narrow trailer wheels sink. He pulls the throttle back. Smoke belches out. I luck behind an wonder how cars will get in the morra. In the middle a the fiel, tractors an lorries to an fro with fencen posts, tables, chairs an bunten. John drives to the tap a the fiel an we unload. He ties the rope round the second crossbar an feeds the other end through the hook. Philip an Denis, lucken on, hauld the planks upright. Another haulds a spirit level against them while he nails posts slanted against the upright. He tightens the bolts to fix the first crossbar to the uprights

'Now, Patrick. Pull the rope a wee bit til it's tight.' I step back, watch the rope liften aff the ground. I keep goen 'til I ken't pull anymore. 'That'll do, Patrick,' John calls as he lifts the second crossbar above head height an pushes a peg in to hauld it in place.

'Anywan got a fork an sheaf?' Dennis esks.

'Well, there ye are now, Patrick,' John laughs as Philip draps them at his feet.

I nod me head an move away. Behind me, a tractor speeds up an down, mowen the grass. Damp clumps appear. A man in wan corner digs out a rectangle for the long jump. He fills it wi' sand an rakes it over. Along one side of the fiel two men set up the high jump. They lay bales a straw for the jumpers to land on. Willie an Hugh, from me class, kerry a bucket a whitewash an brush. They paint white lines for the sixty an hundred yards races; the three-legged race, the egg an spoon race an the sack race. In the distance, a group a men on a tractor an trailer put up sheep netten along the trees an a sheep pen in an open space for the sheepdog trials. I wonder how Shep will get on wi' Daddy the morra.

'Come on. Patrick. Let's go. I hev to see Paddy Jimmy Mor and Joe the Jammer about their donkeys for the Donkey Derby.' I jump aff the tractor at home an John goes to see the men about the donkeys.

I lie in bed, staren at the ceilen. Ivrythen is quiet, apart from the sound a Daddy's whistle an shouten at Shep. It feels lake Sunday today too. It's the Feast of the Assumption an we hev to go to Mass agen.

'Good Morning,' Father Kelly says, without stoppen us at the chapel door this time. After the Bible readen he opens a sheet a paper in his hand. Oh no, not the list from yisterday agen. I luck at Mammy. She tuts an rolls her eyes. Father Kelly raises his voice. He complains at ivrywan that not enough men helped yesterday. He orders ivrywan to tirn up, buy tickets for the activities an encourage the children to take part. He threatens to go into Barney Grant's Pub an hunt the drinkers out. Men, sitten at the back of the chapel, shuffle an whisper. Father Kelly staps an stares. Some leave.

By the time we get home it's half past ten. We hev breakfast. I wander round the fiels. I sit on the rocks at the back a the house. In the distance, an engine roars. I luck round. A car speeds through the village a Killourt. Its tyres screech at Packie Bann's corner. I wait for the bang. The car continues to roar. I ken't see it. I watch for it to pass the gap in the whin bush hedge. It's Conn Big Mickey in his silver Rover 2000 that he's brought home from London where he works on a builden site. Daddy says he's showen aff. He comes home ivry year for *The Fifteenth*. I think of me brother, James, when he went to England. He came home after a week because he was homesick. He said he wudn't do it agen.

The beepen a horns make me tirn towards the chapel. Tractors wi' trailers kerryen sheep, bales a straw an long planks puff out blue smoke. Lorries, hooten their horns, kerry tables, chairs an plastic boxes. People, singen an shouten, stand near the edge a the trailers. *Big Tom and The Mainliners* showband music plays from a car. I run back to the house. 'Can I waalk to the Sports?'

'Can't see why not, as long as you're careful and you're back here by five o'clock.' Mammy says, openen the press. 'Here, take this. You'll need to buy a ticket,' handing me half a crown coin. 'You'll have enough left to get yourself a wafer of ice-cream from John Joe's van.'

I run to me room an grab me coat. Yes! An ice cream. I'll be on me own. I ken do what I want. Daddy'll be too busy sorten Shep an the sheep to watch me. I hope Shep doesn't behave for him. I run out the front door. I sprint to Mary Anne's shop. I think about the time I tauld her that Daddy had died. She said she'd tell him but he niver said anythen. Maybe she tauld him to say nothen. I waalk past John Joe's shop, me school, an The Crossroads Hotel where Mr. Quigley drinks. He'll be in there now an then he'll scrounge a lift to Barney Grant's.

I turn right along the bog road. As I get nearer the voices are louder. Children call out an laugh. The glare from the sun on the windows of lorries shine through the whin bushes. The tap of the Thrown the Sheaf frame sticks up above the hedge. The rope sways in the breeze. I breathe in the smell of sausages cooken somewhere in the fiel. I'm not sure whether I'll buy a sausage or ice-cream. I might hev enough money left to buy both. Mammy wudn't lake me to get a sausage. She doesn't trust any butcher apart from Bertie Boggs in Malin Town, even though he's a Protestant.

'In ten minutes, Father Kelly will open Sports Day from the lorry here,' announces a lady from a loudspeaker. 'Then the events will begin. Buy your programme here.'

I peep through the hedge. I ken't see anythen apart from a man waven cars into parken spaces. I kerry on. Over the cliff, on the other side a the road, the fishen boats bob up an down on the waves batteren Port Mor pier. A flag flaps from the tap a the coastguard station on the cliff behind. Blue fishen nets dangle over the sides a the boats an chains hit the cement steps. The smell a fish an engine oil fill the air. Two rows a caravans, parked on the gravel beach opposite, cover what grass there is. Bins overflow as usual. The lids shake. Children splash at the water's edge. They scream when the waves rush in. Daddy calls the families Protestant tinkers because they come from Derry for their holidays.

I head to the ticket table at the gate. The mud an gravel from yisterday are covered with planks. Water oozes out from the sides. They wobble when I step on them. 'A shillen,' A man says. I hand him the half a crown an he gives me one shillen an six pence change.

'Gi'me yer wrist,' stampen a blue circle on me skin. 'If ye need to go out agen, just show me yer wrist.' I take the change an rush to the Throwen the Sheaf area. A rope fence wi' a narrow gap, circles it. Men stand round waiten for somewan to hev a go. The sheaf a rushes, tied at the tap, bottom an middle wi' orange baler twine, lies between the uprights. White stuff oozes from the end a the stalks. The heads, full a seeds, bend towards the grass. A new fork with clean wood an shinen prongs, stabs the sheaf in the middle.

'Come on, hev a go, Mickey. Ye nearly won last year,' me brother John says.

'Getten too auld far that malarkey now,' says Mickey Big Willie shaken his head.

'Go on, Tom,' he says nudgen him on the shoulder. Tom smiles. Ivrywan cheers. He edges forwards. Ivrywan claps. He grabs the fork an stabs it into the sheaf at a slant. He shuffles his feet, opens an closes his fist round the new clean handle. He bends his knees. He lucks at the crossbar. He lucks at the sheaf agen. He lifts it an lets it balance. Wi' a loud puff, he swings the sheaf above his head. It flies through the air. Water drips onto his head. The sheaf hits the bar. Tom jumps back. He shakes his head. 'Ye ken do it,' somebody shouts. 'Give it another go.'

Tom tries agen. The sheaf hits the bar. He shakes his head an waalks away.

'Ye hev one go left. Tom. Third time lucky,' John calls. 'Take a step back and ye'll get a better angle'. Tom throws for the last time. The sheaf bounces a the tap of the bar. The bar wobbles. The sheaf rolls over an thumps to the ground. Tom slides his flat cap back. He nods an waalks away. Ivrywan cheers. John pulls the rope another fut an waits for another man.

I luck up the slope towards the sheepdog trials. Daddy stands outside the fence with Shep lyen by his feet. Two men stand beside him. I waalk to John Joe's ice-cream van. *99s 6d* a notice says. I buy wan an luck at Daddy. He hasn't won. He waves his stick in the air an bangs it on the ground. He storms aff. Shep follows, his nose touchen the grass an his tail between his legs. He'll batter Shep when he gets home. He'll tie a tin can to his tail, lake he did wi' the aulder sheepdog, Laddie. This time, I'll make sure I get the can aff afore he runs away.

I waalk back to the races. Father Kelly waalks up an down the side of the fiel forcen boys an girls to take part. They line up for the sprint, egg an spoon, three legged, an sack races. Some laugh an shout. Some hev long faces. The adults cheer them on. I want to join in but I don't want to. I know I ken run fast. I cud win. I'd get a prize. Mammy'd be pleased. I don't lake people watchen me. I waalk away.

'Patrick,' John shouts. 'Ye want to see me in the tug o' war?' I follow him to the long thick rope stretched out on the grass. A red flag sticks up beside a blob of red paint in the middle of the rope. About two yards on either side, pieces a orange baler twine are tied round it. The Malin Head an Clonmany teams approach. The men, wearen heavy boots, pick up the rope. They space out a yard apart an kick their heels in the ground. They spit on their hands an grip. A man on the Clonmany team towers over ivrywan. He brushes his red hair back an stares. It's Danny McGonagle. We'll never win. He pulls for County Donegal, an won the all-Ireland competition last year.

'Take the strain, men,' the referee calls, standing by the flag. 'Move a wee bit to me right. The paint an flag hev to be touchen. When the baler twine reaches the flag, I'll raise me hand an shout to stap. Wan, get ready. Two, take the strain. Three, heave.'

The men pull. They grunt. They slide. They dig their heels in. The Malin Head men heave. The orange twine nearly touches the red flag. The referee gets ready to raise his hand. With wan almighty pull, the Clonmany team forces the Malin head team to lose their futen. The men slip an faal. The referee raises his hand. Clonmany wins.

Docks

I pulled the bent A4 pad from the front pocket of my holdall. I tapped the top of my pen on the sheet. I wanted to write.

To my right lorries, laden with freight, disembarked. They groaned their way back towards the A75. Cars with trailers and roof racks followed. To my left dock drivers swivelled their cranes three hundred and sixty degrees. They drove forwards and backwards loading freight containers as fast as they could. A security van with an orange flashing light patrolled. A group of Scottish, Irish and English accents walked past. Go away. I wanted alone. I wanted peace. I wanted silence. I tapped the pen on my lips. Did their fathers die without speaking? The accents faded. I had nothing to write.

Corn

After the ploughen an harrowen, the fiel is ready for sowen corn an barley in April. My father unhooks the corn fiddle from the barn wall, oils the rusty metal plate an checks for mice holes in the sack cloth. I help him to lift a bag a corn. I stumble. I put the fiddle an bow into the wheelbarrow. I push the wheelbarrow to the top of the fiel. He shuffles the fiddle onto his stomach, tightens wan canvas strap round his waist an another over his shoulder. With a final shuffle the fiddle hangs near his dungaree's belt. He opens the mouth a the little sack above the plate. I lift the bucket a corn seed above me head an with me eyes half shut I tip it in. He shuffles agen. With a quick shuffle of the sack he pushes the mouth under the shoulder strap. 'Git back or ye'll git hit in yer eye.' I step behind. He pushes the fiddle bow to an fro to make sure the round flat spinnen metal plate with tiny wings turns. 'Ready. Stay well clear aff the corn.'

He flicks a metal lever at the bottom a the fiddle to let the corn drap down. He pulls an pushes the bow from side to side lake playen a violin. He strides down the fiel taken long strides. His wellingtons sink up to his ankles in the saft ground. His right arm moves right, left, right, left as the corn seed showers the soil to his right, left an in front of him. About halfway he stops, wipes his forehead, shuffles the sack an waves to me to kerry another bucket a corn to him. I tip it in. He nods. I head back to the tap of the fiel, fill the bucket an wait. Once he reaches the end he takes four long strides to his right an heads back up the fiel maken sure the shower of corn doesn't overlap the last row.

When the fiel is finished Daddy links up the harrow to Joey, our big black stallion. He steers the horse up an down the field wi' long reins from behind the harrow raken the corn into the ground. Seagulls hover an squawk. Joey has to make a wide circle to tirn round at the end. Daddy whips him wi' the end of the reins.

Daddy unhooks the harrow an links the metal roller to the harness. They waalk up an down the fiel until the corn is buried an the surface smooth. The surface is broken wi' horseshoe marks in straight parallel lines. Crows settle an peck. 'Shooo,' Daddy bellows from the tap of the field, clappen his hands.

He hammers a fence post into the centre of the fiel. He nails a crossbar to it. He fits an old hat an coat to the frame. The sleeves dangle. The crows hover at a distance squawken. Daddy laves. The crows hover. Two or three land at a safe distance. He borrows a rifle from Jack Merchant across the river. He sneaks behind the hedge, rests the gun barrel over it an takes aim. The crows fly away. Wan crow flaps its wings, scatters dust an goes still. A wing stands up. Daddy clicks the barrel and empties out the bullet. He shuts the barrel and rests the gun over his shoulder. Wi' a piece of baler twine, he ties its legs together an loops it round the horizontal wood. He heads back to the barn. The crow swings. Its wings stick out. They shake in the breeze. Its head dangles. The other crows settle in the fiel next door.

The corn begins to shoot green leaves an stalks, growen up to a yard tall by July. The stalks round the edges of the fiel are thin, short an pale. There are bald patches where the seed hasn't grown. Further in, the stalks are thick, strong an a deep green colour. They hev knots lake knee joints ivry few inches. Even though they are strong, they snap.

As the days pass, the pale green turns to a dull yellow. The heads droop. Nearer the middle of the field the dark green fades at different speeds, in different places, to a light green. A golden yellow appears. The heads of corn thicken, splitten the chaff. The bottom half of the stalks turn yellow afterwards. The patches of green become less as they change to yellow. More an more yellow emerges until the whole field is a sea of golden heads swayen in the breeze. Daddy waalks into the middle of the field. He pulls a few heads from day to day to check if it's ready for cutten. If the corn is saft an milky it's not ripe. If it's hard an dry it's ready. After strong winds or heavy rain some a the crop faals flat afore it ripens. Crows feed on it. Daddy cuts it out wi' a scythe afore it knocks over more corn an rots.

When the crop is ready, an the forecast is fine, the harvest begins wi' Daddy sharpenen the scythe wi' a sharpenen stone. He rubs both sides of the blade so fast an so near the edge I'm scared he'll cut himself. I try to do it lake him when he isn't lucken but I ken't. He grabs the two handles on the shaft an swipes the scythe from right to left. He grunts. The stalks faal against the shaft. They lie flat to his left. He steps forward. He swipes agen. He grunts agen. I follow two yards behind him. I gather a handful of stalks. I separate them into two lots, cross over the heads of both bunches an twist them into a knot to make a straw strap. I lay the stalks out in a straight line. If the strap lucks too short I add another handful to the end. I gather an armful a corn stalks, haul them upright an tap them on the ground to make the ends even. I lay them across the strap. I pull the strap tight an twist the ends into a knot. I fold the knot ends under the strap. If the strap breaks I make another wan. I do it quickly so Daddy doesn't see me. I hide the old strap in the sheaf an lay it on the edge of the field. The thin stalks cut into me palms. Me fingertips sting from pushen the strap under the knot. I open an close me fists to ease the pain. Me back aches. I stand up after drappen the sheaf. By the time we get to the end of the fiel there is a row of sheaves an a stubble path wide enough for the tractor an reaper. 'Git the reaper blade in the barn. Sharpen it. The stone's lyen on the binch. We'll get the reaper out the morra.'

I lay the six-foot long wobbly metal blade on two buckets tirned upside down. Its twenty-four triangular teeth, as big as me hand, are rusty. I put a corn bag over the teeth before I sit on the bucket wi' a leg on either side of the blade. I grip the sharpenen stone wit both hands an rub the edges of each tooth, maken sure I stroke away from me body. I grind an grind til the rust is gone. The tooth is warm. I start the next wan. Me fingers ache. I open an close them. I move the bag. I slide the blade forward. I kerry on til all the teeth are shinen. 'There's two or three loose wans.' Daddy rests the blade on the anvil, checks the teeth an hammers the loose rivets. The hammer thumps. Their heads flatten. The anvil clinks. 'Git some auld oil an brush it on.'

I pour old tractor engine oil from a five-gallon drum into a tin box. I coat the blade wi' a paintbrush wi' bristles stiffened from roof tar. The oil dribbles on me hands an under me nails. James pushes the blade into the reaper. He moves it back an forth to make sure it slides smoothly. He pumps grease from the grease gun into the nipples on the cog casen underneath the metal seat. The tractor revs in first gear. Black smoke belches out as he tows the reaper along the edge a the corn. The blade disappears as it slithers to an fro. I ken't see it but the faalen stalks tell me where it is. Daddy sits on the reaper. The stalks faal against his rake. Every two or three yards he draps the bundle. I follow behind maken straps. He doesn't let me tie these sheaves because they are bigger an heavier. Neighbours Jack, Robbie, Dennis an Roger tie them. Our two cats sit nearby on their hind legs waiten to pounce. The roar of the engine, the clatter an smell of the warm oily blade fill the air. Everybody rushes to clear the sheaves afore the reaper comes agen.

About eleven o'clock Mammy appears at the tap of the fiel kerryen a basket. She staps halfway an heads back to the house. She reappears with a large tin teapot. She puts a few sheaves in a circle an places a tablecloth in the middle. She spreads out sandwiches an cakes. 'Tea!' Ivrythen's quiet apart from the thunderen waves of the Atlantic. We sit on the sheaves. She passes round cups a tae an plates a sandwiches an cake.

After the tae we continue cutten the corn til six o' clock. We gather the sheaves a similar size into stooks a four. We lean them against each other so that they hev a wide square base to stand up, let the rain run aff, an allow air to flow through. We pull a handful a stalks from wan sheaf an tie it round the four near the tap. The stooks are placed in straight rows so that the tractor an trailer can come along later to load them. Crows come agen an land on the tap a the stooks. Daddy sets up more scarecrows. He hides in the stooks. He shoots more crows. Five crows dangle.

After a few days the heads a corn begin to droop. They soak up rain. With heavy wind an rain the stooks faal over. We have to re-build them fast. Sometimes the cows break into the fiel, knock them over an trample the corn into the ground. When there's no-one round Brendan an I play hide an seek between the stooks.

In the autumn The Killourt River, separaten our farm from Jack Merchant's farm, overflows into a deep hollow in wan of our fiels. It runs along a narrow shuch. Salmon swim into the salmon hole there. Daddy catches them in a net an hides them in the stooks. He tells ivrywan he puts salt on their tails an they stay still. People laugh. After a couple of weeks of dry weather, the stooks are ready for gatheren into stacks. 'We need to git the harvest in afore the weather breaks,' Daddy says to James. 'First thing the morra. It'll take us most a the day.'

In the mornen they hook up the tractor an trailer. It's Saturday. I'm allowed to drive the tractor between the rows. Daddy an James walk along the side of the trailer. They fork the sheaves up to Dennis. He starts by layen the sheaves along both sides of the trailer with the corn heads facen inwards. He lays more rows in the centre an continues til the trailer ken't take anymore. As he starts each new row he places the sheaves a couple a inches in from the edge a the previous row so that the sides are slanted inwards to prevent the load from faallen aff. 'Aff to the tap a the fiel now.' I drive the tractor, lucken round at Dennis sitten on tap of the load.

'Kerry on, nice an aisy,' says Dennis rubben his forehead with his cap an spitten out his tobacco. I aise the throttle as we approach Daddy an James. They build a large base for the corn stack. They hammer posts into the ground two yards apart, an two fut tall, to make a circular fence. They nail boards along the tap. They lay auld pieces of wood an planks inside the fence. They trample whin bushes an rushes from the Moss Fiel. They flatten ivrythen wi' their forks til the surface is even an sturdy. 'Fire away, Dennis,' James shouts.

Dennis, standen on tap of the load, stabs the sheaves wi' his fork an throws them into the centre. Seeds of corn scatter. Daddy an James lay the sheaves round the edge a the round base wi' the corn heads facen inwards. They continue til a row is complete an then start another row further in til the whole base is covered. A second outer row is started with the end a the sheaves overhangen about an inch to allow rain to faal aff. As each row is added up to head height the circle becomes a little larger.

From here to the tap of the ten fut high stack they tap the butts a the sheaves wi' their palms to create a slant lake slates on a roof. Each new row becomes smaller an smaller til there's only enough room to stand. I rake up the sheaves that faal apart so they ken be used to make straw ropes to tie down the stack. Daddy an James climb down a ladder. They step back to check the stack isn't slanted. The base has flattened. It still allows air to flow. They rake the stack to get rid of loose straw. Wan of them climbs the ladder agen to catch sheaves a rushes forked up to thatch the tap half a the stack.

The final job is to make straw ropes. I haul a hook an Daddy bends a handful a straw in half over the blade. I tirn the handle. The straw twists. He feeds another handful onto the end. I kerry on tirnen the hook an twisten the straw. Each time he adds straw I step back. The rope gets longer. It sags. It brushes the stubble. Me arms ache. Me wrists hurt. 'Step back quicker,' he grumbles. Me back twinges. Me shoulders drap. Me arms go weak. I want to stap. 'Pull more. It'll break if ye don lift it aff the groun.'

When Daddy thinks the rope is long enough he rolls it into a ball, kerries it up the ladder an lets it roll down the other side. James ties wan end near the bottom. Daddy pulls the rope an hauls it tight. James ties the other end. By evenen all four ropes are tied an the loose straw is forked onto the trailer. I drive back to the barn.

The followen mornen the crows return. Daddy hangs another dead crow on the stack. He checks the ropes an tightens them as the stack settles an the ropes stretch.

By September the old straw in the barn is nearly at an end. Daddy has to wait a few days for Danny Shioche to come with his threshen mill an baler. Daddy has to thresh wan stack of corn in the mill in the barn to feed the cattle. He links Joey to the long metal shaft that sticks out through the wall. The mill drum creeks. Its metal teeth turn. It speeds up. It roars. Dust scatters. Joey walks round an round the circle for about two hours wi'out anywan leaden him lake he's done for the last five years. I stand near James. He forks sheaves to Daddy standen in front of the metal drum. It's moven so fast I ken't see the teeth. He slides the sheaves towards the teeth wan by wan. They crunch the straw. The drum groans. Bits of straw fly. Dust scatters. 'What ye doen? Get the hell outa here. Ye'll lose an arm.'

I run to the back. The mill pushes out the loose straw. The loose corn faals down a chute into a bag attached to hooks. Robbie stands waiten to change the bag. Dennis forks the straw to me. I trample it down by the wall. The forkfuls land on me head. The pile gets higher an higher.

I kerry on tramplen til me head reaches the roof. I swipe away the cobwebs an dust. I trample so much I lose balance an faal over. Dust clogs me nose. I blow. Black muck comes out. Me mouth is dry. I spit black. Bits of straw slide down me back. They itch me skin. Me eyes sting. 'Where ir ye, Patrick? Ye luck lake a scarecrow?!' I wave me arms an laugh. I kerry on tramplen.

Daddy feeds the last sheaf into the drum. The drum goes quiet. I slide down to the floor. We waalk outside. Daddy an James wipe their black faces. Bits of straw dangle from their head. Chaff clings to the hair on their arms. They snort, splutter an spit.

Danny Shioche is so busy threshen everyone's corn that he ken't say for sure which day he'll come. The neighbours talk about how long it will take him to finish.

'Aal be wi ye, Willie, the morra about eight,' Danny says on Friday evening. I smile an rub me hands. I ken't remember the last time Danny came on a Saturday. He's always been an gone afore I got home from Quiggy. If Daddy won't let me near the mill in the barn he won't let me near the big thresher an baler.

Just afore eight o'clock a tractor engine roars. I run to the front door. The gigantic blue Fordson Major tractor wi' red wheels an silver grille on the front crawls past Mary Anne's shop, pullen the red thresher an baler. The three machines are so long Danny ken't tirn into our lane. He unhooks the baler. Black smoke hovers over his head as the tractor climbs the brae in front of the house, pullen the thresher on its four wheels. It lucks as tall as the house. He slows down, lucks backwards an forwards to check that he has enough space. He revs agen. The tractor an thresher disappear into the fiel behind the house. The noise fades. I wait. Danny re-appears. He links up the baler. Another belch of black smoke shoots into the air. He tows the baler up past the house. Daddy steps up beside him an lays his two forks on the tap of the baler.

Dennis, Jack an Robbie arrive. They grab forks from the barn, rest them on their shoulders an head for the fiel. Mammy prepares sandwiches an tae in the kitchen for the elevenes at half past ten. I sneak out of the house. Danny pulls the thresher alongside the two corn stacks. He checks the spirit levels on both axles. If the thresher isn't level he levers a wheel aff the ground an places a board underneath. He pulls the brake an kicks blocks of wood against the tyres. With much moven backwards an forwards, he lines up the baler so that it links into the straw feeder a the thresher. He fits a heavy thick canvas belt round the enormous metal wheel a the baler an slides it onto the smaller drum wheel a the thresher. He puts a second belt over the tractor pulley wheel, an another wheel on the thresher. He reverses the tractor inch by inch tirnen it right an left to line up both belts an tighten them. He crouches down, shuts wan eye wi' his cheek touchen the belt. 'Aal ready an straight now,' he calls. 'Stand well clear, aal a ye.'

He pulls the handbrake, presses the throttle an pushes the pulley wheel gear stick. The belts swish. The wheels tirn. The thresher shakes. Its drums groan. The metal baler head shaped lake a horse's head pounds up an down. Crunch. Crack. Danny runs an staps the tractor. The thresher an baler groan to a slow halt. 'Jasus Christ, who put them damn forks in the baler? It cuda wrecked ivry fecken thing.' Danny clambers on the baler, picks out the smashed handles an bent fork prongs. He flings them as far as he can.

'Oh, Jasus, Mary an Joseph. Me new forks,' Daddy shouts from the tap of the thresher.

'For Christ's sake, Willie,' Danny shouts. Daddy bows his head an tirns away rubben his chin. I waalk round to the back of the stack an start laughen. It serves him right. I hope Dennis, Jack an Robbie make fun of him. I hope they tell Mammy.

Danny starts the tractor agen. He raises his arm to warn ivrywan. James stands on tap a the stack ready to fork sheaves to Daddy. They ken't hear. They wave to each other. Dennis stands by the corn outlets, waiten to change the bags when they're full. Robbie an Jack stand at the end a the baler to catch the square bales a straw. They load them onto the trailer. I scoop away the loose chaff from the bottom a the thresher wi' a rake. 'Right, Patrick, come wi' me wi' this load a bales,' Jack calls when the thresher stops. He drives to the barn. We stack the bales in steps so that we ken lift them up high wan row at a time.

It's six o'clock. The sun is faden. The wind from the sea is getten colder. Danny folds up the belts from the thresher an baler. He hooks the machines up to the tractor an drives them past the front a the house. I stand an watch ivrythen disappear past Mary Anne's shop. Daddy herds the cows into the byre. I go to me bedroom. I finish the long multiplication questions Quiggy gave us an learn aff by heart, an the thirteen times table.

Quiggy

I lift the curtain. Daddy waalks past me bedroom window kerryen an aluminium bucket full a milk. The froth clings to the edge as the bucket sways. He'll put it on the drainen board next to the bucket a water that James has kerried from the well.

In the kitchen Mammy scoops the milk out a the bucket wi' a cup. She pours it into me glass bottle. She squeezes in the wooden cork wrapped in tissue. White bubbles hiss. 'Here you are. Put it into that sock on the table.' I hauld it to feel the heat an slip it into me school bag between me Galtee cheese an ham sandwich, an books. I tighten the two leather straps. Mammy pours the rest a the milk into a large jug an places it on the bottom shelf in the fridge. I luck out the window. Daddy pours three buckets into the tall creamery can. He lifts it onto pieces a wood on the back a the Massey Ferguson. He ties it to the back a the seat with a piece of orange baler twine. He lets the five cows out. They waalk along the midden wall, in the same order ivry day, into the Homes Fiel. He follows wi' a stick in his hand an drags the aluminium gate tied to a cement pillar wi' baler twine. He shuts it against a wooden post. He stands his stick in a barrel. He drives the milk churn to The Square Toe where the milk lorry collects it.

I pull on me duffle coat an sling the leather strap over me shoulder. As soon as I tirn the corner a me bedroom the wind flaps me hood. I pull it over me head, pull the cords and tie it. The door a Mary Anne's Shop is shut. There's no light on. I want to go in an get a sweet from her when I come home. Michael Paddy Brian's sheep dog lies in the doorway a his white house, as usual. I walk past slowly so the dog doesn't bark. I feel me bag to make sure the bottle hasn't faalen over.

I stand by the front door a Saint Mary's National School wi' the boys from me class, waiten to see if Mr. Quigley'll come. 'Get in your playground,' shouts Mrs. Monaghan followen us round the corner.

'Ha, ha, ha ,' Danny laughs. 'Luck at them trousers. Where'd ye git them stupid things? I stare at them. I hate the trousers Mammy got in a parcel from New York. The leather patches rub me knees. Maybe I ken rip the leather. Mammy won't be able to repair it. I won't be able to wear them to school anymore. I cud blame Liam an Danny. No, she'd come into school agen. Mammy'll make me wear them ivry day. 'Luck. Luck at the trousers.' I start to cry. I rub me eyes.

'Straight line, everyone,' Mrs Monaghan screams, 'in you go.' She stares, her cane tucked under her oxter. It's the same cane she had in the infants. I remember its sting on me palm. I rub me palm with my thumb.

She follows us into the school and waits at the cloakroom door. 'Toilet, quickly,' rattlen the glass door. 'Out before I come in an cane the lot of you!' We speed along the corridor into the classroom.'Right, your work is to copy one page from your book in your best handwriting. I'll be back in a few minutes to check if you've done it properly between the red and blue lines.'

'Mrs. Monaghan, I do the ink wells ivry mornen for Mr. Quigley.'
'Get on with it quickly. Mr. Quigley'll be here any minute.'
'Mrs. Monaghan, I'm also the fire monitor with Francis an Gerard. Can we light the fire?'
'No!'. She walks to her classroom next door laven the doors open.

I scoop four spoonfuls of black powder into a jug an fill it wi' water. I stir till all the powder is soaked up. I wait for the bubbles to settle. I pour it into the inkwells. I hev to be careful not to spill any. Mammy tauld me aff last time when I had black marks on the sleeves of me white shirt. I want to tell Daddy that I do the ink. If I esk Mammy she might tell him.

Paddy Kelly dips his nib in his inkwell an flicks it. A black spray flies through the air. I bury me head in me arms hopen it'll miss me. I feel the damp on me neck. I rub it. Black spots soak into the page of me exercise book. I turn the page. Damp stains cover it too. I fill me pen an flick it at him. Paddy laughs. Francis an Hughie join in. Ink splatters on our desks, books, an the map hangen from a bent rusty nail in the cracked plaster. It staps when it reaches the wooden pole glued along the bottom of the map. 'The map!' Shouts Roisin.

'It's yer fault,' Danny whispers pointen at me.
'No. It wasn't. It's him,' I point to Paddy Kelly.
'No. You're te blame. Ye filled the inkwells. I'll tell Quiggy.'
'Good on ye, Paddy,' Tony interrupts.
'I seen 'im throwen the ink.'
Quiggy'll cane me. They'll lake that. They'll say I deserve it because I'm taking the test.
'Just ye wait. Ye'll see what Quiggy'll do.'

Mrs. Monaghan's footsteps clatter in the corridor. We go quiet. 'Well, let's see how we're getting on with our writing,' moven along the desks. 'Hmmm, you all need some handwriting practice. My infants are better. Cathleen, stand at my door and watch the infants for me. Right, watch me. Remember the *a, e, i, o, u* and the other small letters stay between the blue lines,' she says, writen them on the blackboard. 'Watch how I make sure the *l, b, f* and *d* go right up the top red line. Can you see how the *t* only goes halfway up?'

'Yes, Mrs. Monaghan.'

'Good. Watch how the *g, p, q* and *y* go right down to the bottom red line. And what do we do with capitals, Francis?'

'They go up to the red line, Mrs. Monaghan.'

'Get your pens ready. Make sure the nibs are clean. Don't put too much ink on. I want to see five of each letter exactly like on the blackboard. If you finish early copy out a paragraph from your book.'

I dip me pen in the inkwell an tap it. I start to copy her letters. She used to hit me knuckles wi' a ruler in the infants when I didn't write the letters properly wi' the chalk on the slate. Mr. Quigley appears at the door. 'Oh. Thank you, Mrs. Monaghan. Sorry I'm late.'

'I'm just checking their handwriting, Mr. Quigley.'

'Why's the fire not on?' he grunts, lucken at me, Liam an Gerard.

'I couldn't trust them, Mr. Quigley, so I told them to leave it.'

I want to go to the toilet to check me white shirt in the mirror. I don't want to esk him. I'll luck when we go out to the coal house. Quiggy puts his hands into his coat pockets. He takes a box of cigarettes out of wan an slides it along his desk. From the other he takes his silver lighter wi' the lid that clicks shut. He puts it on tap a the Sweet Afton packet. He slumps into his chair an slaps the register open. He calls out our names, boys first. I stare at his desk. Liam an Danny stare at his desk. We luck at each other. I cud steal them. Mr. Quigley wudn't question us because he'd be embarrassed. He'd think he'd lost them. He'd rummage round school an along the road. He'd go back to the pub an esk. I smile. Maybe I cud hide his cigarettes in the bushes on the way home. I ken't take that risk. Liam an Danny'll threaten me to keep the packet. Mr. Quigley wud cane me if he found out. He'd tell Mammy an Daddy.

'Get out your reading books.' We lower our heads an glance at each other. He rests his forehead on his hands. I tilt me head towards the map of Ireland. I squint. The ink has faded into the different colours of the counties an their names in thick black letters. Francis an Paddy luck at me an point to him. They sneer. 'For God's sake. Get this fire on, you three. Do I have to tell you everything?'

Francis, Gerard an myself crouch behind his table an chair. We clear out the grate wi' a shovel an brush. We slide the ashes into a bucket. I wipe me lips. We tiptoe out to the coal house. I run into the toilets. I ken't see any ink. Mammy wud've kilt me. I run to the coalhouse. I luck through the small window. It's black with dust an covered in frost. I wipe the corner. Mr. Quigley waves his arm back an forward as he wipes the blackboard wi' the old cloth. He sneezes. We head back. I kerry an armful a brown tirf. Tony kerries the bucket a coal. Francis kerries pages from *The Derry Journal,* an twigs. Everybody sits in silence doen the long division sums on the blackboard. We scrunch up the paper. 'Be quiet, will you,' Mr. Quigley grunts.

I put the twigs on tap a the paper. Gerard adds the brown tirf. I strike a match. We luck at Mr. Quigley. We open *The Derry Journal* an hauld it tight against the wall across the fireplace. 'Move it up a wee bit for a gap,' he says. 'Watch out for the flame.' The pieces a newspaper curl up, go brown an burst into flame. The twigs crackle. Francis puts pieces a coal on tap. The smoke thickens. We splutter an screw our eyes. Me face stings. We clear up round the grate an head back to the coalhouse wi' the buckets.

Mr. Quigley is standen wi' his back to the fire when we return. The fire howls. The flames lick the blackened cement. 'Ok, you three, copy the sums on the board for homework quickly. I want you all to finish them at home for tomorrow.' He grabs the bundle of dog-eared hymn sheets from the windowsill an shuffles between the rows. He slaps them on our tables.

'After three. One. Two. Three. *Adeste Fideles laeti triumphantes,*' he bellows in his croaky voice, rubben the sweat from his forehead. 'Sing up, Doherty. Can't hear you! For God's sake, you amadans, listen to me, sing it with me.' He picks up the cane from the blackboard ledge and waves it: '*Adeste Fideles laeti triumphantes, Veníte, veníte in Bethlehem, Natum vidéte, Regem Angelorum: Veníte adoremus, Veníte adoremus Veníte adoremus Dóminum.*' We practise the hymns sitten. We practise them standen behind our desks. We practise them standen in a straight line.

When the bell rings at twelve o'clock, we line up behind the girls by the classroom door. 'Right, Siobhan, peg the door back. Off you go.' Once we're out a sight we run as fast as we ken. The girls giggle. They scuttle along the corridor to the toilets. We dash to the other side lake Daddy's young calves let out for the first time. We come to a sudden stap at the door. The bigger boys push to the front, grab Hughie an push him away. Mr. Quigley appears wi' a lit cigarette in wan hand an a cup of coffee in the other. 'If you don't line up quietly I'll have you all back in the classroom,' his voice boomen along the tiled floor an the high ceilen.

He stands by the window opposite the toilet door. He stares out breathin in his Sweet Afton. He blows out grey smoke through his nose lake our bull snorten. The cup a coffee rests on the white-painted wooden sill. Ash piles up in the clear glass saucer. Two boys go into the toilets as two boys come out. I put me face up to the frosted glass. Crash! Me head smashes against the glass. Pieces shatter an scatter on the floor. Mr.

Quigley jumps round. Coffee splatters down the front a his white shirt. It's the same white shirt he always wears, with the yellowish collar. 'What in God's name have you done, Doherty?' his black-rimmed glasses slippen down his face, his eyes bulgen an coffee shaken over the edge.

'Don't know, Sir. Nothen.'

'What do you mean, nothing? Look at it. The mess. You've broken the flaming window, you fool'.

'But, but it's not me fault, Sir. Somebody pushed me.'

'You'd tell me anything, you would. Just you wait till I see your parents.'

I think of Daddy's bulgen blue eyes an red neck. He won't care about me face. He won't want to know who pushed me. Mr. Quigley's neck reddens. I rub away a tear of blood tricklen down me face. He pulls a crunched up handkerchief from his trouser pocket an pushes it into me chest. I press it against me face. I hand it back. He shakes his head. 'It must've been him, Sir,' pointen to Francis behind me.

'Shut up, boy.' When he shouts 'boy' I think a when Mammy came into school the last time. Not another canen. He'll frighten me. He'll threaten me. He'll laugh at me. He'll make fun of me in front of the others again.

'Gerard, get the brush and pan from the storeroom.' Mr. Quigley pushes them into my chest. He stares at me as I sweep up. I rub me eyes with me sleeve. 'Get into the classroom and sit there.'

Mr. Quigley's cigarettes an lighter are still on the table. He follows me in. He tells me to eat me lunch. He picks them up an goes outside. I step up to luck out a the window. I see his head moven past the window. He stands at the corner. I watch the boys playen football. They shout an cheer in the playground. The football bounces aff the wall. I count the thumps against the cement. He shouts somethen. It nearly hits the window. The girls squeal an laugh. Their skippen rope hits the cement.

I think a when me brother Dan kicked the ball an broke the window in the barn. He ran an hid. Daddy tauld Cahir he'd buy him sweets if he tauld the truth about wha Dan a done.

I imagine I'm kicken me ball against our barn wall between two buckets as hard as I ken so it'll bounce back. I pretend I'm Mattie McDonagh playen for County Galway. I want to hev a green jersey an green an gold socks lake him. I want a size five football lake him. I don't want to esk Mammy. The thread between the leather pieces a me size four ball is broken. The stones in the wall break it. I use wan a Mammy's thick needles to mend it. I don't tell her. The tube is punctured. I tried to mend it wi' Daddy's bicycle repair kit but the patch slides aff when I push the tube back inside. I don't pump it up anymore. I push in bits of *The Derry Journal* until the ball is as hard as I ken make it. It hits the wall an drops. I get fed up kicken it, an runnen to get it.

'Right, everyone, line up.' I ken hear across the playground. 'We're practising the Confirmation questions again this afternoon. Learn them off by heart. I'll be testing you in a minute.' I stare at the sheet.

After the Confirmation questions we read an do more handwriten. Me hand still shakes. 'Francis and Gerard, are you nearly finished?'

'Yes, Mr. Quigley.'

'Well, seeing it's such a nice afternoon, do you want to finish off that weeding you started yesterday?'

'Yes, Mr. Quigley.'

'It better be good for when Father McGoldrick comes next week.'

'Yes, Mr. Quigley,' sneeren at me as they waalk past.

Father McGoldrick. He'll shout at us if we give him the wrong answer. If he starts at the front a the class lake the last time he'll esk me question four. I'll practise four, five an six to make sure. I luck at the sun shinen through the window. Me hair is warm. I want to be outside wi' Tony an Gerrard. I think a them crawlen on their knees from bush to bush pullen the long rushes wi' their bare hands lake we did yesterday. The rushes were aisy to see wi' their tall shoots. I made a St. Brigid's cross with them an hung it in the sitten room for Mammy.

Their roots were long an difficult to pull out. Me hands stung from their slippery roots. I split the rush open by runnen me fingernail the full length a its skin. A white, spongy liquid oozed out. We piled the rushes into small haycocks an rested against them. We kept as low as we cud because Mr. Quigley spied on us. My knees hurt from the rough ground. The thorns from the whin bushes pricked me skin. Their twisted roots dug into me knees.

The bell rings at three o'clock. 'Here. Take this home,' handen me a letter with ''Mr. and Mrs. Doherty'' written in black. He stares as I put it into me bag. I shut the door an run down the corridor. He'll blame me. He won't blame Francis because he drinks wi' his Daddy. I want the waalk home to last forever. I want to run away. I don't know where I'd go. I plod along the road, feelen the ridges on me forehead an cheeks. I press the tissue on them. The more I press the more they seem to flatten. Watery blood stains it. I pull a branch danglen from a tree. The leaves are green an floppy. The end is cracked from the storm. The knots an twists luck lake Daddy's stick but his is auld, dry, an stiff. I whip the scutch grass, choppen the heads a the stalks. Sap seeps through the green bark onto me fingers. I thrash an thrash until me arm aches. 'How d'ye lake that, Mr. Quigley? Speak up, boy, I ken't hear ye. Shout at me agen an I'll give ye the worst hiden ye've ever had,' I tell the grass.

I beat the grass so much the roots appear. Bits of bark dangle. The bare wood sticks to me palm. I fling the branch over the hedge. A sheep runs away. It's long mucky tail swings from side to side. The red roof a Crega comes into view. Behind it the tap a Inishtrahill is covered in mist. Daddy said he knew the last people who left the island.

I'd lake to get a boat from Port a Roman an sail there. I open me bag. The long brown envelope lies on tap of me books. Mr. Quigley's neat joined-up handwritten takes up most a its length. Mammy hates brown envelopes. I tirn it over. I hope the flap is tucked inside. It's stuck down. I bend the envelope back an forth. Small crinkles appear. I aise me small finger along the edge. The paper peels open. The glue leaves a dark brown strip. She'll know I've tried to open it. I pat the envelope hard between me hands but the edge keeps curlen up. She'll tell Daddy. I could rip it open an throw the envelope away. She won't know. I'll just give her the letter.

I feel the outline a the paper inside. The piece a paper is so small for such a big envelope. If I dillydally anymore I'm goen to be late. I fold the envelope in half, maken sure the ripped side is facen inwards. I place it inside me Maths book. I ken't see anywan at the house. I luck at the fields. The potatoes are beginnen to cover the drills. Daddy must be in the hay fiel at the back. He said last night he wanted to gather in the hay today afore the weather breaks. I crouch along the whin bushes. A rabbit shoots out. I tiptoe into the hallway. I shut the door so the handle doesn't squeak. I head straight to me bedroom an rush to the dressen table mirror. Three scrapes run from me eyebrows up to me hair. No matter which way I pull me fringe I ken't cover them. A thicker scrape runs from me lips to the bottom a me ear.

'I heard you, Patrick. I've got your dinner ready,' shouts Mammy from the kitchen.

'I'm on my way.'

I search through her creams, lotions an powders on the dressen table. I rub talcum powder over the cuts an check the blood is hidden. I open the kitchen door. Not that salty bacon agen. That big barrel in the barn that Packie Paddy Brian filled with the pig he kilt with a sledgehammer, an cut its throat.

Mammy drains the potatoes into the sink an puts the pot back on the cooker. The letter. I forgot the letter! I run back to the bedroom. I stuff the letter into me pocket.

'You had a good day then, Patrick?' loweren the potatoes, bacon, egg, an Bisto gravy onto the table. I cough. I say nothen. I rub me forehead. I look at the floor an slide into me chair. 'You got a headache?'
'No.'
'I've been rushed off my feet all day, you know. Daddy's out gathering in the hay. He nearly went to get you at lunchtime.' Thank God, he didn't I think to meself.
'My poor feet. I think I'll sit down for a wee while with a cup of tea before I fall down.' I ken't remember the last time she sat wi' me. I move me head. Me neck aches. I take me hand away from me forehead to hauld the knife. I keep me head down.
'Oh Jesus, Mary and Joseph. What's happened?' Before I have time to answer she puts her hand under me chin. Her cup of tea clatters onto the table. 'It's that Francis again, isn't it?'
'No.'
'Well? What then?' I pull the envelope from me pocket an slam it on the table.
'What's this?' tearen open the envelope. 'It's a bill. What have you done, Patrick? Tell me. Tell me the truth.' She pushes the chair back wi' her hips, graten its legs on the linoleum floor. She slides her cup away. She folds her arms. She crosses her legs. 'You'd better be quick before Daddy comes in.'
'Twas Francis. He banged me head on the glass in the toilets.'
'What was that for?'
'Dunno.'
'Well, you better have a good explanation. You know what your Daddy's like,' pullen me to the sink. 'Bend your head back. I'll get some Dettol. You'd think Mr. Quigley would've put a letter in. Did you not tell him who pushed you?'
'I tauld him it was Francis but he wudn't listen. He doesn't lake me anyway.' I glance at the kitchen clock. It's a quarter to four. Daddy'll be in for his tea soon.
'That Mr. Quigley's useless,' she says.
'He came in late agen an Mrs. Monaghan had to come into our class.'
'I'll come in in the morning. If he isn't there, I'll go straight to his house. Poor Mrs. Quigley with her weak heart.'
The noise a the tractor becomes louder as it approaches. I head to the window. Daddy's long grey strands a hair flap. He takes his hand aff the steeren wheel to flatten them. They flap agen. The back a his brown-checked shirt an the rear wheels disappear round the corner. The chuggen fades. Silence.

'Luck! I've told ye ivrythen. I'm not lyen. Francis pushed me. T'was definitely him. He was behind me.' When I tirn round, she's not there. I rush along the hallway. It seems longer an narrower. I close me bedroom door an tirn the key. I head to the mirror. I move me face closer. The cuts are swollen. They sting when I frown. I sit at me table to begin me homework. I wait. The clatter a Mammy's shoes on the cement footpath outside me window fades as she rushes past.

It's gone four o'clock an there's still no sign a Daddy. He shud go past the window any minute. He'll take aff his wellingtons. He'll bang them together an hang them upside down on the wire rack afore he comes into the house. I tilt me head backwards. Me head aches. I open me school bag an start the long division questions. Daddy follows Mammy wi' his head down. Pans clatter. I wait. The back door opens. Daddy scrapes me dinner into Laddie's bowl. She comes out a her tin hut coweren as she approaches the mashed potatoes, bacon, egg an gravy.

Wan time Daddy tied a rope round her neck an beat her wi' a stick. He tied a tin can to her tail to stap her runnen away. I ken still hear her yelps as she ran as fast as she cud up the road. I felt sick. I wanted to run after her, take aff the string an cuddle her but he'd hev hit me too. I felt rage. A week went by an Laddie hadn't returned. Daddy searched the fiels, the boiler house, the barn, the byres an the roads. He esked neighbours but they knew nothen. He didn't tell them the full story. He didn't tell Mammy.

I stare at the page of long division questions. Mr. Quigley always tells me not to check the answers in the back of the textbook. All me answers for the first five are right. I finish the last five. The last one is wrong. I don't change it in case he thinks I'm cheaten. I laugh to meself when the boys say they've worked out all the right answers. He'll get them to do them on the blackboard. He'll hev the cane ready.

It's five o'clock. The kitchen door creaks. Footsteps shuffle outside me bedroom door. Me back stiffens. Me hands grip the copybook. I swallow hard. The handle clicks. 'Leave him alone, will you,' Mammy shouts from the end of the hallway.

Daddy's footsteps fade. The kitchen door shuts. I wait to see him comen out the back door. 'He's gone. You can open the door now. Please open the door.'

'No,' bangen my fist on the table. She doesn't reply.

'Are you still there, Mammy?

'Daddy won't touch you. He promised he wudn't. I told him what you said.'

'Leave me alone.'

I want to speak to Daddy lake that. He'll think I did it on purpose. I'd lake to push his head into the glass. 'What are you going to do then?'

'Homework.'

'And then what?'

'Bed.'

'Bed? It's only five o'clock for God's sake! What about your supper?'

'Don't want any.'

I roll the key between me fingers an tap it on me book. Daddy walks past me window. I wait. Silence. He'll hang round the fiels til dark. He'll come in. He'll stick his head in a western an stay tight-lipped til bedtime.

Mammy's footsteps fade. I want her to cuddle me. I want to feel her arms round me neck. I want to lay me head on her shoulder an cry. The sun glares on me window. I squint. I close the curtains. Tears trickle down the side of me nose. I whimper lake Laddie. The door knocks. I flinch. I gawk at the handle. It doesn't move. 'Mammy says yer not comen out?'

I don't reply. Silence. His footsteps shuffle along the hallway.

'Patrick, get your supper,' Mammy says in a low voice.

'Don't want it.'

'You'll be starving. Just open the door, will you. Stop being so stubborn.'

'No.'

'Right. You'll have to have it cold. It's on the floor.'

I wait until seven o'clock. I peep through the curtains. The sun sinks at the far end a the field. The cows saunter along the ridge, wan after the other, stoppen from time to time to graze. Their tails seem to be flicken the sun. Two cows head aff, chewen their cud. They lie in the shelter a the yellow whin bush. They sit side by side watchen the sun sinken behind the rocks. The others join them. I'd lake to be a cow. Maybe not. He'd hit me if I didn't give enough milk. I'd kick him hard. I'd kick him so hard he'd hev to lave me alone. I cud be a bull. Chase him. Stick me horns in him. Fling him up in the air. Stamp on him when he faals. Laugh at him beggen for mercy.

I button me jacket an pull the collar up round me neck. The bucket at the side a the fire is still half full. Two firelighters lie in their box. A box a matches rests on the mantelpiece. A pair a tongs an a poker hang from two hooks on the matchen metal stand that Mammy lakes to polish with Duraglit. I fall asleep.

Daddy's shouting at the cows wakes me in the mornen. The gate clatters at the back a the house. They moo. I get dressed an tiptoe to the kitchen. Mammy stares at me from the sink. 'Let's look at you,' benden towards me. 'Hmmm. It's dried up quite a bit. I'll dab some Dettol on. Here, get your cereal. You'll be hungry.'

The backdoor latch rattles. Daddy staps. He stares. He steps towards me. I luck away waiten for the slap. 'What the hell wur ye doen?' I luck at him. I luck at Mammy. 'Ye'll come wi me on the tractor this mornen.'

'He's comen!' somebody shouts. Mr. Quigley's grey hair bobs up an down. He approaches the gate. He stamps on his cigarette. He splutters. Mammies an daddies hang round the playground wall an chat. They stap. They stare as Daddy draps me aff. We run back into the playground an line up without speaken. Quiggy stands in front a us. His red eyes stare. We mustn't annoy him. With a nod a the head, an a swipe a his hand, we waalk inside in a straight line. I sit in me desk. I stare at the classroom door ivry time the front door bangs. I wait for a knock. Mr. Quigley marches up an down between the rows a desks readen out the Confirmation questions. We read the answers. He reads the questions agen. He asks each a us to read out the answer. 'Take this sheet home and learn it. I'll test everyone of you in the morning. Take out your hymn sheet now and stand up.'

He sings 'Adeste Fideles laeti triumphantes'. We join in.

Martin sings 'Adeste fiddles, let us triumphantes.'

Quiggy staps. He stares. He listens. I kerry on singen tryen not to laugh. 'Venite, venite in Bethlehem. Natum videte. Reem Angelorum.'

'Sing up,' he bellows, walken between the rows.

Just afore playtime a loud thump makes me jump. Mammy's green hat moves on the other side a the glass. 'Where in God's name were you yesterday?' marchen into the classroom wi' a tremble in her voice, her lips tight an teeth clenched.

'Don't you threaten me, Mrs. Doherty,' waggen his finger.

'I'm not threatening you. Not yet anyway.'

'Out,' he's pointen to the door.

'Just answer my question, will you,' raising her voice.

'For your information, I was ill yesterday. Mrs. Monaghan, next door, kept an eye on everyone.'

'So she can see through walls, can she?'

'There's no need to be sarcastic.'

'You're nothing but a bare faced liar. Ill? You were no more ill than I was. You were in The Crossroads. Don't deny it.'

'How do you know where I was?'

'Daddy saw you waiting at the door. You're as bad as the rest of them.'

'No need for that.'

'I'll report you.'

Mr. Quigley wags his finger near her nose. She doesn't move. I peek round. The boys stare at me. They clench their fists. They snarl. I feel lake a rat trapped by dogs in the corner a the barn. They'll get me after school. They'll batter me agen. They'll threaten to tell Mr. Quigley about the map. They'll blame me for maken Mr. Quigley angry. The neighbours'll gossip. He'll get his friends' sons to batter me. He'll buy them a drink.

'Nobody speaks to me like this.'

'Well, it's about time somebody told you a few truths. I want the best for Patrick. He's bright enough to go to the college and get a good job. For God's sake, sort yourself out or ...'

'Or what?'

'He's going to another school. And I'm not paying for any pane either.'

I think a when Mammy sent my brother Kevin to The Christian Brothers in Cork. Please don't send me. I want to esk him why Mammy sent him away but he's in Dublin now. I glance from the book I'm pretenden to read an stare at her. She lucks at me an heads down the corridor. 'Just remember! I'm going to report you.'

The slam a the main door echoes along the corridor an into the classroom. Mr. Quigley lucks out onto the football fiel. I luck at me book agen. I try to learn *Adeste Fideles*. I glance at him. He opens the tap part a the window an flicks the butt outside. He tirns. He staps afore he opens the door. It bursts open, shaken from tap to bottom. The panes rattle. 'What are you looking at?'

We stare at our books. Nobody speaks. 'Get on with your work.' He frowns an squeezes his eyes shut. He marches past me to the back a the classroom. The cane on tap a the cupboard. He's goen to hit me. He snorts. Bang. The cane whips the side a the cupboard. Swish. It flicks his trousers. Out a the side a me eye I see the scuffed toes a his black laced shoes. The cane wallops the tap a me desk. I grip me head. My elbows squeeze against me cheeks. The cane breaks. Half a it faals on me book. 'Well, you like to tell your Mammy about school, don't you?' I don't reply.

'Don't you?' The cane thumps the desk agen. Me head sinks into me chest. Me hands quiver.

'Yes, Sir.' He slides the cane aff the desk

'I'll be watching every move you make, boy. One step out of line and you'll get the worst beating you've ever had,' stoopen over me. His grey stubble an stinken breath force me to tirn away. I'm not sure if it's the beer or cigarettes that smell the worse. I don't reply. 'Do you hear me, boy?'

'Yes, Mr. Quigley.'

'I can't hear you. Speak up so we can all hear you, boy.'

'Yes, Mr. Quigley.' He moves his face away.

He groans as he straightens. With a long sigh he waalks to the blackboard, tappen each table wi' the cane. He fills the board wi' long division sums. The creases on the back a his tweed jacket run from side to side. The split curls up. The sleeve slides up his arm. The padded shoulders rise as he writes. 'Get on with it,' tirnen towards us.

He sits an stares at me. I open me book. A tractor chugs past. I want to luck. That's Daddy. Where's me pencil? I shake me book. I lift the lid. I close it. I glance to me right an left. I lift the lid agen. 'It's under the desk,' Francis whispers. I stretch me leg. I roll the pencil under me shoe. I start to copy the questions. The pencil slips through me fingers. They sweat. I rub them on me jumper. I try agen but notice a damp mark on the page. Me shirt collar sticks to me skin. I rub me finger along it. I shiver.

'When you're finished the sums get the class reading book out. Read the next chapter.' I begin to read *Rotha Mór an tSaoil* about Mící Mac Gabhann's life in the Gaeltacht in County Donegal. Francis whispers. I can't make out what he's sayen. I luck back at him.

'Turn round.' I luck at Mr. Quigley. He stares. I wait for the cane. He doesn't move. I stare at the page. I don't want to read. I luck sideways at the boys. They stare out the window. They cough. They shuffle. I glance at the clock. Mr. Quigley opens *The Derry Journal*. He slaps the pages. He sighs. He glances at the clock. He goes into the corridor, shuts the door an lights another cigarette. Mrs. Monaghan approaches him. I can't make out what they're sayen. She lowers her head an squints through the pane at me. I know they're taalken about me. With wan last puff a smoke he flicks the butt out the window. He splutters an comes back in. I luck at the clock. Five minutes. He shuts the newspaper, picks up the register an slams the cupboard door. 'Right, put your books away. We'll see about that chapter tomorrow. Off you go.'

Mr Quigly grabs his cigarettes an lighter. We waalk along the corridor. I grab me coat from the cloakroom. Liam an Danny snigger. Mr. Quigley follows us down the path to the gate. Mammies an daddies stare. He tirns right towards The Crossroads.

I run as fast as I ken past John Joe's shop. He stands at the door staren. When I reach the pumphouse I start to waalk. A hummen noise comes from inside. There are no windows. I don't know what it's for. Two seagulls balance on the electric cable between the ESB poles. The cables hiss in the drizzle.

'Well, what happened today?' Mammy esks as I open the kitchen door.

'We did a lot of long multiplication an readen.'

'I hope you got them all right,' poken the potatoes wi' a fork.

'He didn't check them.'

'He better do it tomorrow or I'll be in again.

Woodbines

'Make sure you do every question properly in your test today'. Mammy tells me. 'It's your only chance of getting into The College.' I want to tell her to stap. 'I don't want Margaret and Elizabeth getting into the convent and you not getting into The College.'

I want to go to The Tech. I cud learn woodwork an metalwork. I want to become a carpenter lake me brother John in Chicago. I want to make a wooden shelf an a little box lake me brother Dan made when he was a The Tech. I'd be able to use chisels, hammers, screwdrivers an drills. I want to learn how to measure an cut wood. I'd lake goen to the tech ivry day. I'd be with the pupils from the Malin Head school. They wudn't have teased me if Mammy hadn't forced me to try for the college. We'd be together in the same class. We'd make things together. We'd be friends at playtime and on the bus. Mammy niver asked. I was goen to the college lake me brother Cahir and that was that.

I remember what Cahir told me about Father Campbell hitten him with the leg of a chair, an Father Gallagher maken him bend over an hitten him with a hurlen stick. Then there was Father O'Reilly liften him by the sideburns, an Father McKenna wanten him to become a priest. The worse bit was the older boys ducken his head down the toilets.

I ken't understand why he'd not tauld Mammy. She might've changed her mind about me. His heavy school bag, the thick textbooks sticken out as he waddled up the road past Mary Anne's shop, swappen it from wan hand to the other. He always lucked sad. He spent ivry evenen in his room. She wants me to be as good as him. He's laven an goen to Maynooth to be a priest. I don't want to be a priest.

Daddy doesn't want me to go either. He wants me to stay on the farm. I want to get away from Mr. Quigley. I hate Mammy comen into school. I'm afraid she'll come into the college too. Liam an Danny. Father Kelly shouten. No friends, no football an all the exam practice. I wonder if Margaret an Elizabeth feel as lonely as me about the test. I'm the only boy doen the test.

Everyone moves seats. Margaret sits in the front seat, Elizabeth in the second an me in the third. Mr Quigley hands out the exam papers. It's lake a big book with two staples down the middle. The size of it! Me hand shakes as I open it. I'll niver do all this in an hour an half. I stare at the front cover. There's some writen across the tap in Irish. I don't understand it. There are two thick lines across the middle for my name. 'Get on with the questions on the board, everybody. When you've finished get out your reading book.'

'Right Elizabeth, Margaret and Patrick, put your name on the front in your best handwriting.' I luck round. Liam an Danny stare at me. They make fists. They cover their mouths an whisper. I know they'll force me to smoke agen on the way home. I stare at me name. I think a what Mammy said. I flick through the pages. It's arithmetic on the first, the next page long division an long multiplication. Then fractions an compound interest. On the last two pages there's a story an ten questions.

Mr. Quigley waalks up an down between the three rows a desks, stappen an checken what ivrywan's doen. The boards squeak. My desk tilts a little under a loose board. Nobody speaks. He puts more tirf on the fire. He sits down an rests his chin in his hands. Sparks spit an blast upwards, sideways an forwards. The flames rise. The cinders crumble into the grate. He waits.

'Ok, your time is up.' He picks up our papers an checks the writen on the front cover. He puts them in a large brown envelope an locks them in the brown cupboard behind the door. 'Put your jotters in your desks, everybody. It's nearly a quarter to eleven. I'll let you out early,' he says lucken at the alarm clock on his desk while we lift the desk lids.

'Line up,' he says, holden the brown wooden knob. He twists it. It squeaks. We hev to follow him out ever since Francis pushed me head into the glass. The boys don't pick me for football anymore. I sit in the shelter. Margaret an Elizabeth skip an laugh wi' the other girls. I want to join in. The boys wud laugh at me.

Mr. Quigley waalks round the playground wi' a cup of coffee in wan hand an a cigarette in the other. He lucks at the white strand in Gort na Mullen. The smoke swirls round his head. He wafts it away. He leans over the wall an splutters.

'Right, line up. Playtime's over. We're going to go through the Confirmation questions now.' 'Right, Patrick, question five. What was Pentecost?'

'Pentecost was the holy event of the descent of the Holy Spirit upon the apostles, ten days after the Ascension and fifty days after Easter. Pentecost is the birthday of the Church.' I get the answer right. He moves on, demanden more answers. Later he makes us stand up to practice singen *Adeste Fideles,* again. He staps beside Francis. Tony doesn't make any jokes. We all sing standen up. He makes us sit down agen.

'I'm going to read out five questions about the renewal of baptismal vows that the Bishop will ask you on your Confirmation. You answer "I do" to all of them.' He reads out the questions. I don't understand them. Some of them are long. He staps to take breath. He kerries on. I'm not sure when I hev to answer.

'Then there's the anointing with chrism. The bishop will call you to the altar with your sponsor. Your sponsor will put his right hand round your neck onto your right shoulder and the bishop will make the sign of the cross on your forehead with his thumb. He says a prayer and you say "Amen". I don't know what he means by chrism an sponsor.

The boys line up in twos between the rows a desks. The girls go behind. 'I'm going to be Bishop Farren. The person on your right, put your right hand on your partner's right shoulder. You both come to me and I'll make the sign of the cross on your forehead. You then move away. Then we'll swap over and practise with the other person.'

Francis puts his arm on me shoulder. He pushes me wi' his hips. He laughs. I push back. We're third in the queue. I watch. I listen. The wans in front a me turn away. We step forward. Mr. Quigley stares at me. The whites a his eyes luck yellow. He lifts his right hand. His thumb is brown. The nail is long an dirty. His breath makes me screw up me face. His collar is yellow on the edges. A loose thread dangles from where the middle button was on his jacket. His fingers press on me head and his thumb rests on me forehead. They shake. He wiggles his thumb. It feels greasy. We turn away. We swap. Francis squeezes me shoulder. We follow the girls. Mr. Quigley pulls a crumpled hankie from his trouser pocket an wipes his forehead. We swap agen. We queue up agen.

'We're going to do this one more time and practise the pioneer pledge prayer. This is the prayer the bishop will ask you to repeat after him at the altar. You promise to refrain from alcohol for life. He will pin a badge to your lapel which you must wear always. Repeat each line after me. Speak clearly:

'I promise, not a partial, but a total abstinence, for my whole life.

Help me to be true to my promise. Make me a generous apostle of Your Sacred Heart.'

Ok, you can put your things away.' As soon as the door opens, Liam an Danny rush a the classroom. I get me coat from the cloakroom. I luck through the window. They stand a the school gate lucken back. I sneak out the side door we're not allowed to use an run across the playground. I jump over the wall an run as fast as I can.

'Luck. He's over there,' somebody shouts.

I run faster. Liam an Danny chase me. They get nearer an nearer. They grab me bag near John Joe's shop. They pull me coat. I faal back onto the tar. 'Get in there an get us some Woodbine or we'll tell on ye.'

They'll tell Mr. Quigley I stole cigarettes if I don't go in. He'll tell Mammy an Daddy. Then Daddy'll hit me. Liam an Danny will batter me. I peep through the shop window. I ken't see anybody. The back door is shut. I sneak in the front door. They stand outside. I tiptoe round the counter. I push past a tea chest an a bag a potatoes. 'Come on. Hurry up, will ye,' Danny whispers.

I ken't see him. The Woodbine in green an white striped packets lie on the shelf. Blue an white packets a Player's Navy Cut sit beside them. Red an white packets a Marlboro sit on tap of the Player's Navy Cut. Plugs a backie lake dog poo lie beside them. I think a Jack Merchant across the river chewen bits a it an spitten it out through the few black teeth he has left. 'Quick,' hisses Liam.

I swallow hard. Me hands sweat. Me collar sticks. I grab three woodbines from the packet. I glance at the back door. As I pass the tea chest me trousers catch a splinter. It scrapes me leg. The back door squeaks. The boys run. I crouch an run after them to the crossroads. I luck round. John Joe stands at the door. I rub me chin.

'Where's the Woodbines?' esks Liam.

'Here,' as I open my palm. They're bent an cracked. I try to straighten them up but the tobacco starts to faal out.

'Get the matches, Liam,' shouts Danny, panten.

'Heven't any.'

'Behind the red brick,' he points to the wall. Liam takes the matchbox out a the plastic bag. He strikes a match. Another match. Then another match. The rough damp side a the matchbox begins to peel aff.

'Stap,' I shout. 'Ye'll end up wi' nothen left. Give it me.' I put two matches between me hands an blow until me cheeks hurt.

'It'll niver work.'

'Well, we do it in Glentogher when we're cutten the tirf.' I blow agen until I'm out of breath. I strike wan match on the fresh side a the box. A spark shoots out. A flame flickers. It dies. Nobody speaks. I put the matchbox between me hands an blow.

'Try it now,' says Liam comen closer wi' his half Woodbine between his lips. I strike the match. He stoops an breathes in hard. 'Keep breathen in. It's lighten. Kerry on.' He splutters. He bends over, splutters agen wi' his hands on his knees an spits out a mouthful of gunge. 'Oh be Jasus, me bloody throat. Here, hev a wee puff,' wheezen.

'Don't want it.' I hand it to Danny. He pushes me hand against me face.

'Take it or else.' I twitch me eyes. Me fingers begin to feel warm. He pushes the butt against me lips. I spit out the loose bits a tobacco. I breathe in.

'Take a proper puff, ye clown. Push it out yer nose.' I throw the butt away. I want to vomit. He punches me mouth.

'Oh shit, Miss McGuinness's comen,' Liam whispers. We juke behind the whins. Twigs break. No-wan speaks. She'll tell Old Quiggy.

He'll tell Mammy. She'll smell it on me clothes. She'll tell Daddy. 'She doesn't know us. She's only here for a couple a days in the Infants.'

Her shoes clatter on the tarmac. Her black coat flaps. Her brown handbag swings from her shoulder. The wind blows her hair over her face. She flicks her hair back an tucks it under her collar. Her shoes become louder. Her laces sway with ivry step. She looks at her watch. She sighs. She passes by. The noise a her shoes fades.'Ok now. She's gone,' Danny whispers edgen his head above the whins. 'Guinness is good for ye!' he shouts poppen his head up. 'She'll niver find out,' he sniggers, ducken below the whins.

'She'll find out from Quiggy,' I tell him, shaken.

'She ken't prove anythen.'

'He'll know it's us.'

Liam jukes above the whins. 'She's comen back. Run. Run.' We run along the hedge, benden as low as we ken. Our bags bounce over the grass. After a safe distance we luck round. She stands at the end of Dock's Lane wi' her fists on her hips. She lucks round. We wait. She waits.

'What are we goen to do. Daddy'll batter me if I get home late.'

'Shut up, will ye. Yer nothen but a cry baby,' Liam whispers.

'Aye, bloody teacher's pet,' adds Danny clenchen his fists. 'Yes, Mr. Quigley. No, Mr. Quigley. Three bags full, Mr Quigley.'

'She's goen,' Liam says. We edge our heads above the bushes an watch her storm aff.

'We'll be in trouble the morra. Quiggy'll cane us.' Danny takes aff his coat. He runs at me wi' his fists closed.

'Go on, Danny,' urges Liam. 'He thinks he's better than us cos he's goen to The College.' Danny punches me lip an kicks me hip. I faal. They laugh. I crawl away as fast as I can. He kicks agen. I scramble to me feet. I run away limpen. I hold me hand over me mouth.

'Ah, ye big saftie. Run home to Mammy. I'll get ye the morra.'

I run along Dock's Lane past John Eddy's house. I keep runnen because his sister shouts at ivrybody. My brother James told me she chases people wi' a stick. I stop at the shuch. I smell me hands an me sleeves. They smell lake Quiggy. I don't know how he ken breathe in so much smoke an breathe it out through his nose. The smell a his breath still makes me sick. I want to be sick. I wash me hands in the shuch. They still smell. I pull some grass an rub it between me hands. I sniff them. They smell better. I take aff me coat an swing it round. I kerry on waalken, swingen me coat. I put me coat on as I get nearer the house. The ESB poles stand in a straight line all the way along Port a Ronan an up the hill past Pat Shields' house. A thick black wire loops between them.

Pat's dead now. Nobody lives there. The chimley's faalen in an the thatch is black.

I think about the day I ran home from school an waalked past his house. The front door was open an his dog lay there but I ken't remember whether it was black or black an white.

I remember me brothers Willie an John helpen to load the poles onto the pier from a boat at Port a Ronan. They were so long an heavy it took four men to lift them on an aff the lorry. Me brother James tauld me that when I was a little boy he remembers me watchen a big lorry wi' poles tryen to tirn round at the front a our house. He laughed when I esked why the lorry cudn't tirn round at its home.

The holes for the poles were so deep I cudn't see the bottom. They men wud shout an heave til the pole was upright an then they'd pound in concrete. After a couple a days a man wud step on the metal prongs sticken out an climb to the tap. He'd hev a thick leather belt round the pole an his waist. Tools dangled from his tool belt while he bolted the wire to the pole. I remember counten twenty-five poles.

Mammy tauld me I was a baby when electricity came to Crega. She said the house was allowed only wan light an wan socket in each room. She said she remembered waalken a mile to Barney Grant's shop to refill the square glass batteries for the radio. I remember the water level goen down from day to day. I want to know what it must hev been lake to hev no light at night. I suppose she lit the tilly lamp that Daddy uses now for checken the cows afore he goes to bed.

I taste the blood on me lip. I rub it. It stings when I close me mouth. I waalk past Paddy an Biddy Collins. The door is shut. The front of the house lucks so white now wi' the fresh whitewash. I think the salt from the sea will soon make it crack. I luck at Roger's sheep. The fence he put up is still standen an the sheep are grazen in the fiel. Ivrythen is quiet round his house. His bicycle isn't by the front door. It's Thursday. He'll hev gone to The Crossroads. I luck towards its tall white gable in the distance at the junction of New Road an Malin Head Road. Behind me the Atlantic stretches as far as I ken see. The tap a Inishtrahull Island is hidden in the sea mist. The waves crash against the rocks senden showers a white spray into the air. Seagulls squawk over rubbish rollen round on the water's edge.

Ahead a me there are fiels a different shapes, sizes an shades a green. A few are bare after the potato diggen. They luck lake the blankets Mammy made from her auld brown skirt, a grey dress from Auntie Ellen in New York, a tweed coat an dungarees from Uncle Philip in Detroit, me black school overcoat an green cardigan. Roger'll hev cycled past

Crega, Mary Anne's Shop an Big Denis' yellow house to pick up his dole cheque from the post office. He'll hev ridden past John Joe's shop an the school. He'll hev stood his bike at the pub door. After getten drunk he'll come home along New Road an turn left at the bridge near the shore. I think a the story James told me about Roger crashing into the bridge.

'He wuz comen home wan night from The Crossroads. He wuz so drunk he cudn't take the corner. He fell aff an fell into the river, bike an aal. He waalked home completely drooked, the waater squelchen outa his boots.'

'Where's the shoppen?' his sister Rose shouted.

'In the river,' Roger replied.

'Where's yer cap?'

'In the river.'

'An where's the bike?'

'In the river.'

I tiptoe in the front door. I sneak into the bathroom. I lift the mirror on the cistern. I hauld it close. Me lip is swollen. I tirn the mirror over to the magnified side. Red water shines over the black blister. I spit into the sink. I tap me lip with a piece a toilet paper. A bit sticks. I spit agen. I waalk into the kitchen.

'Hello, Patrick, just getting your dinner ready,' Mammy says, drainen the potatoes into the sink. She wafts the steam wi' the cloth on her shoulder. I sit at the table, rubben my face.

'You look upset.' I don't reply. She stares at me. 'What's happened to you?' screwen up her eyes.

''Danny Roe hit me.'

'What for?'

'He started fighten wi' me on Dock's Lane.'

'Oh, Jesus, Mary an Joseph. He's a bad article that one. Just like his drunken father. What were you doing there anyway?'

'Playen football. Him an Liam wudn't let me come home.'

'We'll have to put a stop to this,' dabben my lip wi' a cold wet cloth. 'I thought you've been coming home a bit late the last few days.'

Mammy slides the plate a shelled welks, herren an potatoes onto the table. The steam rises above me face. I pick up small pieces a potatoes an mix them wi' the white sauce she makes from the carageen moss I collect from the rocks on the shore. I slide small pieces into the side a me mouth.

Mammy starts washen the dishes. 'When Daddy finds out it was Danny an Liam he'll go mad. He doesn't like them or their fathers.'

Mammy goes outside. I listen for Daddy's footsteps. She returns. 'Go and do your homework. Daddy'll be in in a minute.'

She's tauld him. He'll leather me. She'll take me to school in the mornen. Mammies an Daddies will see her agen. Danny an Liam will see her. He'll cane me an Danny. I sit in me room staren out the window.

'Laddie, Laddie. Come boy,' Daddy calls, droppen the leftovers into the bowl at the back door.

My bedroom door opens. 'What the hell wur ye doen wi' them buggers? They're bad articles. Keep away. I'm tellen ye now. They're nothen but trouble.' Before I hev time to speak his hand thumps the side a me head. Me ear stings. It rings inside. I feel dizzy. He hits me agen on the other ear. I faal to the floor. I scream. He waalks out.

When I get up James an Brendan are standen by the midden wall lucken at me through the window. I stare at them. They stare at me then kerry on whitewashen.

It's eight o'clock. Mammy comes into me room. She puts her arm round me neck. I push her away. I cry. She pulls me close. 'You want to come to the kitchen an sit by the fire with me?' 'No.' She laves. I crawl under the blanket. The fresh mattress prickles me skin. The smell reminds me a when James cuts the corn wi' the reaper. I sink into the saft straw. It crackles. It's warm. There are no lumps or fusty smell lake the auld one. It's getting dark.

My door opens. 'Daddy'll take you to school in the morning. He'll pick you up after school. I'll get him to drive past the playground at playtime and watch. If that doesn't stop them I'll be in to see Mr. Quigley again,' patting my blanket. I stare at her as she laves. Please don't come into school agen. They'll call me sissy, Mammy's pet an Mammy's boy. No other mammies or daddies go into school.

In the mornen Mammy is in the kitchen afore me. 'Hello. Your cornflakes are on the table there.' I pour the milk. Me hand shakes. I don't want to eat. The backdoor latch rattles. Daddy comes in an draps a bucket of milk on the drainen board.

'Hope yiv larnt yer lesson.' I don't say anythen. I luck at the floor an cry. I pull on me overcoat. I close me school bag a books, bottle a milk an sandwiches. I follow him to the tractor and sit on the back seat. We go past Dock's Lane. I ken't see Liam or Danny. Daddy parks the tractor by the playground wall. I still ken't see them. I grab me bag an step down. 'Stay where ye are. Don't move.'

I sit back up. We don't speak. We wait. Liam, Danny an the girls waalk through the side gate into the playground. The boys spot me but say nothen. 'When the bell goes ye ken go in.'

At lunchtime the boys stay away from me. I stand at the side a the playground waiten for Daddy to go by.

I luck out a the cloakroom window at home time. Daddy's tractor is parked in the same place. He's talken to other daddies. I ken't see Liam or Danny. They'll be waiten for me at Dock's Lane. I step onto the tractor. We drive past. I ken't see anyone.

'Well, what happened today then?' Mammy asks.

'Nothen. They didn't speak to me.'

'No need for me to go in in the morning then.' I luck at Mammy. I sigh with relief.

Mr. Quigley tells me I've passed the exam. I think about how long it is afore I lave. I count the days on the calendar. I mark aff each day.

The Border

At half past six a uniformed lady in a high viz jacket, carrying a torch, approached the booth. The crosses turned green. I edged forward. 'Good morning, Sir. Can I have your ticket please?'

She handed me my boarding pass, lounge ticket and a hook-shaped card to hang from my rear-view mirror. I proceeded to the security checkpoint. A man in a blue uniform stepped forward with a clipboard. He noted my car registration. I wound down the window. 'Is this your vehicle, Sir?'

'Yes.'

'Are you travelling alone?'

I stared at him. No, I have three people hiding in the boot.

'Yes.'

A security woman paced towards the back of the car.

'Can you open the boot please, Sir?' My molars began to grind. My jaws tensed. I opened it.

'Did you pack your luggage yourself?'

No. I didn't. It was the cat.

'Yes.'

'Can you open this bag here, please?' I opened the holdall. She bent over and looked inside.

'Are you carrying any weapons or drugs?'

Yes, of course. Would you like to see them?

'No.'

'Thank you for your co-operation, Sir. Please drive to the numbered lanes where you will be directed to park. Have a good trip, sir.'

Memories of boat trips home during 70's-80's had long ago sapped my patience. Officials singled me out for interrogation because my name was the same as an IRA terrorist on the run. My name is the most common name in Donegal. There are a lot of Patrick Dohertys. The fear. The shame. The officials' silent stares. The gawks from others.

I remembered, too, the afternoon in 1973 when my brother Dan and I were stopped in Aughnacloy on the border between County Monaghan and County Tyrone on our way back to Malin Head. Dan's Ford Anglia had stalled and wouldn't re-start. I sat in the front passenger seat while he got out and opened the bonnet. Two soldiers approached us with rifles pointed. They clicked and took aim. 'Move away,' one shouted to Dan who tried to explain that he was checking the battery leads and plugs.

'Get out,' the other shouted to me. 'Hands above your head.'

They marched us at gunpoint to their lookout post. They spread-eagled us against a wall of sandbags. They riffled through our clothes from head to foot.

'Name?'
'Daniel Doherty.'
'Patrick Doherty.' We answered feeling the sandbag on our noses.
'Where you going?'
'Malin Head.'
'Registration?' I looked at Dan.
'ZP9000.' They nodded for us to go.

'Christ, what do we do if it doesn't start?' Dan whispered to me. I looked at him, shrugging my shoulders. He lowered the bonnet and pressed it until it locked. We got in, shutting the doors gently. We looked at each other. Dan turned the key. He turned the key again. The engine started. We smiled. We looked straight ahead.

Potatoes

In February the fiel for potatoes is nothen but hard bare soil from the winter frost or soggy from the half-melted snow. I'm glad it's Saturday. I pull on me boots an gaiters, hook up the blue Ford Dexta an drive to the shore for a load of slat mara. Daddy watches from a distance. He says nothen. I wait for him to come to me. He doesn't. I know I shudn't be taken the tractor on me own.

The Atlantic wind bites me ears an numbs me fingers. The thundren waves force the fresh, brown, rubbery, slippery rods of slat mara with their flat leaves onto the shore. They gather together in heaps on tap of the auld rotten piles on the gravel. I reverse the trailer along the side a the heap so that I ken fork the old slat mara into it with the wind at me back.

I scrape back the fresh rods an stab the graip into the rotten heap underneath. I pull an pull. The rods break. The leaves fall aff. Blue an black insects scurry away. Me nose twitches. The deeper I dig the more rotten the rods are. Each forkful squelches out from the soggy pile. I sling it into the trailer.

In the distance, Francis, who lives in his family cottage near the shore road, rushes along the water's edge, hoppen from rock to rock. He stoops to collect the fresh slat mara still floaten at the water's edge. He drags them along the sand, laven wavy streaks behind. The ripples cover the wriggly lines. He lays the slat mara side by side in bundles ivry few yards. He ties a rope round each bundle. He pulls the rope over his shoulder. It digs into his collar. He bends, snorts an stumbles. He staps, bows his head an stoops. He rests his hands on his knees. His yellow sou-wester hood hides his face. His ripped oilskin leggens flap against his green wellies. After a few breaths he stands upright an pulls another bundle up the stony beach to the dried stack on the roadside where a lorry will pick them up to take to an iodine processen factory.

Daddy used to say his neck was so raw that ye cud see his shoulder blade. He gathers the slat maras early ivry mornen afore the farmers ken arrive to load up with trailer fulls. They need to spread it on the fiels so that it will rot afore the springtime.

When the trailer is full I waalk to the water's edge an pick a fresh slat mara rod. I wash it in a clear pool. I snap the head aff an chew it. It tastes of dulse. Seagulls squawk over the trailer an the hole I've made in the rotten heap. I drive the tractor along the flat beach to the stony tracks. I turn left to climb the stony slope. The rear wheels spin. The trailer wheels flatten an sink. Frances stands an stares. I know I shudn't hev done this. I shud've taken a wider turn lake me brother James does to get a fast run at the slope.

I reverse down the beach to the water's edge. I put the tractor into first gear, pull the throttle back as far as I can an release the clutch. The tractor raises its front wheels. The rear wans spin. The front wans bounce. Come on, ye bugger. Go. Go. Go. The tractor spins along the blue sand squirten water sideways. It bounces over the stony tracks. The trailer sways. Stones crunch. When I get to the tap I ease the throttle. I take a deep breath. Thank God, I didn't hev to fork aff some of the load. I drive the load to the fiel. I hop aff the tractor an open the tailgate. I jump on the trailer. I slide a heap of slat mara onto the soil. I kerry on in a straight line til the trailer is empty.

I drive the tractor back to the house. Outside the byre, Daddy has reversed the stallion, Joey, an cart into the midden. He's forken cow dung into the cart. I drive the tractor past. The trailer bounces over the gravel. The metal axle bangs. Joey bolts in fright. His front legs flail in the air. His eyes bulge. 'Jesus Christ, what ye fecken doen?' Daddy screams at me with the graip in his hand.

I stap the tractor. I wait for him to run at me. He stands an scratches his head with his flat cap. Joey dashes down the lane. The metal wheels bounce over the gravel. Cow dung falls aff. The reins drag. He neighs. He throws his head from side to side. He snorts. When he gets to the end of the lane he staps. Daddy stabs the graip into the midden an waalks towards me. I jump aff the tractor. He heads down the lane towards Joey. 'Wo, wo, wo. Shhhh,' Daddy whispers, tiptoen in a wide circle.

He stoops slowly an picks up the reins, watchen Joey. He tugs the horse. Joey turns. He snorts an stamps his feet. He swishes his tail. Daddy pulls. Joey follows. Daddy coaxes him back into the midden. Daddy piles more dung into the cart. He piles it til he ken't reach any higher. He pats it flat. He tugs the reins an leads Joey past the house to the fiel at the back of the house that James ploughed yesterday. I peep through the whin bushes. Daddy leads Joey into the soft soil. He picks up the reins an whips him. The horse bolts. The cartwheels sink. He whips him agen. Joey snorts. He drags the cart. It sinks more. Daddy whips agen. The axle drags. It digs into the soil. Joey trembles. His legs buckle. His eyes bulge. 'Get up, ye bastard,' whippen agen. Joey groans. Foam covers his mouth. Daddy waalks away.

I go into the house. I want to go out to Joey. I want to rub his long black an white nose. Daddy heads to the barn an returns with a pair of pliers. He heads back to the horse. I sneak out to the whin bushes. He's kneelen by Joey's neck collar. He wriggles the pliers. He pulls. A strap flings backwards. He goes to the other side. The other strap flings backwards. Joey wriggles up on his front legs. They wobble. Daddy hauls the reins. Joey stumbles onto his four legs. He snorts, throws his head in the air, an swishes his tail. Daddy hauls the reins tight an leads him back to the Holmes Fiel. He unclips the rope from the halter. Joey snorts, kicks his hind legs in the air an neighs. He stops, swishes his tail an stares at Daddy. Daddy steps backwards towards the metal gate without taken his eyes aff Joey.

By March the cow dung an slata mara hev rotted into the ground. By April the land is dry enough to plough. James links up the furrow plough. Its sharp shoe cuts through the soil an tirns it over. The slat mara disappears. The tractor groans. I smell the diesel. The rear wheels spin when the plough hits a large stone. The plough jolts. The damp soil shines. The soil cracks. Some faals back in. Worms wriggle. Seagulls hover. They squawk. Some land on the furrow. They gobble the worms. They fight. They shit.

After about a week the fresh soil is dry. James hooks up the disc cutter to the tractor. After a few more days the tractor drags the wooden harrow to create a fine surface. Next, he uses the drill plough to make drills for the potatoes. He lucks ahead to keep the tractor in a straight line. He lucks behind to check the plough. He moves the hydraulic level up an down to sink the plough to the right level. I don't know how he manages to make the drills so straight the full length a the fiel. They are all the same distance apart, the same height, an width. They luck lake the little ridges on the inside a a piece a corrugated cardboard.

In the meantime, I help Daddy to split the Arran Banners an Kerr's Pink seed potatoes saved from last year. He dumps a bag onto the wooden skip. An empty bag hangs on two nails at the narrow end to catch the splits as they faal. 'Make sure you cut straight down the middle between the eyes. If there's no eye the pirties won't grow,' he says over an over agen. 'If they're too wee don't split them.' I check each potato an cut it. The inside is juicy an white. Some hev black spots. 'Throw them into the barrel. They'll do for the pigs.'

We dump the bag of spilts on the floor an cover them with lime. We turn them over with a pirty graip. I don't know why they cover them with lime. I think it's somethen to do with preventen disease. By the mornen the lime has dried into the splits. Daddy cuts a bag into the shape of a satchel an threads a piece of orange baler twine round the edge. He places the bag across his stomach an ties it round his waist. 'Ye'll need to help me do some planten.'

I fill the wheelbarrow with the splits, maken sure the wind doesn't blow the lime into me eyes. He waalks ahead with his spade over his shoulder. I push the wheelbarrow to the tap of the field. He haulds the mouth a the bag open. I drop a bucketful a splits in. He shakes the bag to spread them evenly. 'Enough,' he says holden the bottom a the bag with both hands. He stands at the head a a drill, presses his spade into it with his right foot, an levers the handle forward with his left hand. A hole appears. He picks a split with his right hand an draps it into the hole. He pulls the spade straight up so that the split doesn't stick to the back. A slit across the tap a the drill shows where the split is planted. He takes a step back. He does the same agen an agen until his bag is empty. He staps every few yards an bends backwards. He rubs his lower back. 'Another bucket,' he shouts from down the field.

I waalk along the narrow V shape between the drills tryen not to faal over. We kerry on until the wheelbarrow is empty. I fill another wheelbarrow. When Daddy has planted the three drills of early potatoes James fits the planter on the back a the tractor. There's a seat on both sides. James fills the box on tap with splits. He drives over the flat harrowed soil. The double plough cuts through the soil an makes two drills at once. I sit on wan seat above wan plough an Daddy on the other. I slide a square metal plate. Splits slide down onto a tray. I hold a split in each hand. A bell rings. I drap the split. It faals down the funnel. The plough covers it. The bell rings agen. I drap the other split. Every time the bell rings I drap a split. Daddy does the same.

After a few minutes I've learned to drap the splits in time with the bell. I count the splits to find out how many go into the whole drill but I lose count. The dust from the grips a the tractor rear wheels blows into me face. Me eyes begin to itch. I rub them. I drap the splits faster with the other hand. I hauld me hand over me face. The dust dries me lips. It slides down me neck. I shrug me shoulders. When we get to the end a the fiel James slides the hydraulic level to raise the planter. I rub me eyes an stretch me arm. I wobble as the tractor swings round. He lowers the planter to start another two drills. No dust this time. Daddy'll get it. Serves him right. I wonder if I swapped sides if I would miss the dust. I don't want to esk.

After about three weeks the heads of the potatoes appear. Some grow straight out a the tap a the drill. Some grow sideways. Weeds begin to appear. At the weekend Daddy tells me to hoe between the drills. The drills are long. I want to stap. I want to go into the house. He won't let me. I kerry on to the end. I stap an luck at the two drills I've done. I waalk along the end a the fiel an count the drills. Fifty-four. I start to hoe agen.

Daddy appears at the tap a the field. He starts at the far side. By the end a the day we have finished the fiel. When the weeds have withered James drives the drill plough agen through the fiel molden up the sides a the drills. The stems a the sprouten potatoes disappear. The leaves rest on tap. During the rest a the spring an summer the heads a the potatoes grow taller an wider. Some faal over. Small purple flowers with yellow centres appear.

In September Daddy rips open a plastic bag. He scoops out four shovelfuls a blue powder into a large drum. We kerry buckets a water from the barrel outside the barn door an fill the drum three quarters way up. Bubbles burst. The powder hisses. 'Stir the bluestone well in. Mind ye don't splash yer eyes.'

    I stir an stir with a shovel handle until me arms ache. Splashes land on me fingers. The ends a me fingers tirn blue. Specks a wet powder stick to the side a the drum an the handle. Daddy pulls on his waterproof leggens. He unhooks the tin sprayer from a peg on the barn wall an fills it. He lifts the tank an places it on the bench. With his back against it, he slips his arms through the straps an ties the belt round his waist. He stretches his hands backwards to aise the sprayer aff the bench. He shakes his shoulders. Once he's comfortable, he waalks to the tap a the fiel an begins to pump the long lever sticken out the front. The nozzle at the end a the rubber hose splutters an spits. A blue spray shoots out. 'Keep away from this. It'll blow in yer face.'

    I waalk away an watch. He haulds the nozzle in front an sways it from side to side as he waalks along the drills. The blue spray wets the potato leaves. He walks up an down the fiel until the bluestone is finished. He goes back to the barn an refills. He continues sprayen til all the drills are covered. His leggens shine. After a week the leaves begin to droop.

    By the end a September they've tirned brown, grey an black. Daddy waalks along the drills an pulls some stalks. If they break he knows the potatoes have stopped growen and are ready for diggen. He listens to the forecast after the one o'clock news, checks the weathervane in the boiler house, an chats to neighbours. When he's satisfied that it's goen to be fine for a few days he arranges with Roger, Robbie, Jack, Michael an Dennis from across the river to help.

It's Wednesday. I am lyen in bed. I luck at the clock. It's eight o'clock. I listen. I ken't hear any rain. The tractor engine revs near the barn. Daddy's wellingtons scrape outside me bedroom window. He shuffles along the hallway. My door opens. 'A need ye to help wi' the pirties the day.' He tirns an laves.

Yes! No school. I jump out a bed and pull on me auld weekend clothes. I sit by the kitchen window an gulp me cornflakes. Clumps a dark cloud move over Mary Anne's shop. The whin bushes in the Homes Fiel bend in the breeze. The tractor engine whirrs as it pulls the potato digger up the street at the front a the house. Its metal wheels clatter on the gravel. Its frame shakes. The men follow, kerryen creels that Jack made from sally rods. I dash to the fiel in me boots an wooly jumper. The men stand in twos, spaced out, equal distance apart, along the length a the drill, with creels in their hands ready to gather the potatoes when the tractor has passed.

I join Dennis. James straddles the tractor over the first drill, pulls a long lever at the back of the digger to lower the long bar over the end of the drill. He checks the screen sewn together from auld potato bags to make sure it touches the ground. He puts the tractor into first gear an crawls along. The wheel at the back a the digger with its thick forked spokes turns. Clay scatters. Pirties bounce an roll. They hit the screen an faal.

Seagulls hover. They squawk. As soon as the tractor passes, Dennis an I stoop, pick up the potatoes two or three in each hand an drap them into the creel. We step forward with our backs bent. I dig me fingers in to scoop out the half-buried potatoes. Me fingers ache. Clay sticks under me nails. As the creel gets heavier Dennis an I hauld a rope handle each to lift it forward. It sinks into the fresh soil. Clay sticks between the thin rods. The more we move it, the more the clay cakes on the bottom. Me back begins to ache. When it's full we grab a handle each an lift. Our boots sink. The creel rubs our legs. We wobble to the flattened area an empty it. Dennis bangs it on the ground. Some soil faals off. 'Need to put less in next time. We'll do our backs in. We've a long day ahead.'

I luck down the drill. Four small piles a white potatoes about the same distance apart stretch in a straight line. The men to an fro kerryen an emptyen their creels. 'I think another creelful will finish our stretch,' I say.

'Ay. It should. Need to get a move on to finish afore the tractor comes agen.' We rush back an pick the last few yards a scattered potatoes. I kneel. Me knees sink. I rest on me hips. Me back aches less that way. I rub me hands together. The damp soil blackens me palms. It dries. I wiggle me fingers. I luck to the far side a the fiel. I count forty-four drills.

Dark clouds pass over the hill at Killourt. I hope it rains. It's too late to go to school now. I'll miss French, History and Maths. I lake French with Father Lagan. I'm glad I'm missing History an Maths. The sun begins to shine through. The tractor starts. James starts a new drill.

'No time to sit round. Come on,' Dennis says with a smile. 'Yer father'll be watchen ye.'

I luck down the drill. Daddy stands with the creel in his hand staren at the tractor. He edges forwards as it comes nearer. I jump up. He'd hit me but he doesn't want the neighbours to see. After eight drills Mammy appears at the tap a the fiel. 'Tea's ready.'

It must be eleven o'clock. We finish the drill. The piles a potatoes are taller an longer. We head towards the house. We kick our boots an wellingtons against the fence posts an wash our hands with carbolic soap in the boiler house. 'Sit down an I'll pour the tea. Help yourselves to everything,' Mammy says as she moves round the table haulden a dishcloth under the large tin pot.

'If we didn't hev to ate or slep we'd hev more time to work,' Daddy says, spreaden butter on his bread. Ivrybody gives a little laugh an nods. I ken't remember the last time he spoke at the table. He's getten at me for sitten down.

About four o'clock dark clouds come across The White Strand. The waves tirn grey an churn. The wind rises. I ken't feel the tips a me fingers. Me socks are damp. Me toes are numb. It's goen to rain. We'll hev to stap. I watch James driven to start another drill. He lines the tractor up. Oh no, please don't dig another wan. I want to cry. He staps the engine. 'Need to cover them pits afore the rain,' he calls.

Everybody draps the creels an marches to the trailerful a rushes cut yisterday by the river. We kerry sheaves to the heaps a potatoes. We tidy up the wans round the bottom, slope the sides an spread rushes all the way round an across the tap. We shovel clay over the pit. The clouds get darker. Spits of rain drap. 'We'll need to take the creels into the barn to keep them dry,' Daddy says.

With auld knives an screw drivers we poke out the clay an brush the creels. We tirn them upside down. We wait for the rain but it only threatens. 'We might as well get more rushes for the morra. It's supposed to be dry,' Daddy says.

James hooks up the tractor an trailer. We all jump on an head to the Moss Fiel. James swipes the scythe. We gather an tie them into sheaves. We load up the trailer an take them to the potato fiel.

When the men have gone home I help Daddy to milk the five cows. I watch the clouds moven over the barn an the Moss Fiel. They pass out to the sea. If it doesn't rain tonight I might be able to miss school agen because Daddy wants the potatoes dug as soon as possible. I'll miss English an Science. Mr. Sheridan doesn't have any patience with me because I don't understand Shakespeare. He's stapped esken me anythen.

I hate Science now ever since Father Campbell knocked me aff the stool for not doen a proper drawen a the micrometer.

'Yer stayen home the day agen to finish the pirties,' Daddy says as he comes into me room at half past seven. I know me fingers an back will hurt but it's better than English an Science. I'll miss the homework too. Mammy'll write me a letter to the principal, Father O'Reilly. He won't lake it when he finds out I was gatheren potatoes. He might suspect me a writen it meself.

By four o'clock the fiel is finished. We scrape the clay aff the potato pits an thatch them with a thicker layer a rushes. We dig round the bottom a the pits to let the rain drain aff an pat the clay into a deep layer all the way round.

During the winter I sneak out a the house an waalk along the pits with Laddie, at the weekends, to catch the mice an rats that nest in them. I lake walken with him. I think he lakes it too. He doesn't tuck his tail between his legs when he comes with me. He trots along at me heels. Deep cracks run from tap to bottom a the pits after the frost. Round holes appear an Laddie sniffs at them.

Wan Saturday Daddy wakes me at eight o'clock. I don't want to stand over the skip all day. I wouldn't mind if I was goen to miss school agen. If we don't finish, I'll hev to do the same agen tomorrow even though it's Sunday. I waalk to the fiel. James an Daddy hev scraped the clay aff the pit. The rushes are brown an flattened. Clumps a chewed leaves lie at the bottom. I watch. Laddie stands an stares. James forks potatoes onto the wooden skip with the potato graip. Daddy an meself slide them along the slats. Dried clay falls through. 'Watch out for the rotten wans. They're a bit hard to see. Must get rid a them afore they rot the rest,' he mumbles.

I roll them towards the narrow mouth a the skip. Some squash an faal through. Some squash less an stick to the others. I wipe aff the mess an throw it away. The smell makes me gag. I push the potatoes to the end. They faal into the bag. James forks up more potatoes. Daddy an I kerry on checken them. He doesn't speak. I move from fut to fut. I blow into me hands. Me breath swirls in the frosty air. I tighten me coat round me neck. Me ears sting. Laddie jumps. 'Get it!' James shouts as he dashes aff haulden the graip in the air. He bangs the graip on the ground. He misses a rat. Laddie dashes. It disappears into the whin bushes.

'There'll be a nest somewhere,' Daddy says.

When all the potatoes are bagged we move to the other three pits. We load the trailer an drive the bags to the barn.

During February Daddy waits til he gets word that the potato inspector is comen afore the potatoes are sent to the alcohol factory in Carndonagh. Daddy clears the barn floor. He places the wooden riddle skip with two different sizes of mesh under a bulb hangen from a long purple flex. The biggest mesh is on tap an the smallest on the bottom. Daddy dumps a bag of potatoes onto the mesh. Dust rises. The bulb shines through it. It warms me head. I wipe the damp from me forehead. I blow me nose. Flies hover. I slide the tap mesh back an forth along the inside a the frame. The potatoes spread out. I roll them along. Damp skins appear on some. I rub aff the clay. Others are black an wrinkled with white spots. They squelch into the mesh. 'If they're soft, throw them out.'

I poke them. A thick brown liquid oozes out. I pick them up. I screw up me face. I snort. I throw them into the wheelbarrow. I wipe me fingers on the wooden frame. They smell. The smallest potatoes fall through the second mesh to the floor. We lift aff the tap mesh an dump the big potatoes in the corner. We slide the good potatoes, on the bottom, into new potato bags hangen at the narrow funnel a the skip. When the bag is full he lifts it onto the weighbridge. He adds or takes out potatoes to make the fifty-six pounds weight balance. We fill auld bags to keep some potatoes for planten in the spring. We dump the peoreens into a large drum to boil for the pigs. 'This inspector's a bugger. He'll esk ye to pick out a bag on the bottom row. If there's any rotten ones he'll fail the whole lot,' James says.

Daddy rolls up the mouth a each new bag to make a ridge along the tap. He twists the end into an ear shape an ties a piece a new white string round it. He threads it through a long thick needle, pushes it in an out all the way along. When he reaches the end he pulls the string out a the needle, pulls it tight an passes it through the hole in the factory label. He grabs the end a the ridge an wraps the string round the other ear. He ties a knot. He lifts each bag by the ears an lays it flat on wooden planks. By midnight all the bags are stacked to head height. I luck across the skip at James an Daddy opposite. Dust hovers round the bulb an up to the roof. Their breath cuts through it. Their faces shine. Their hair hides in the dark. I luck out the barn door. Frost is shiny on the tractor bonnet. The streetlight shines from the byre roof. A white frost covers the midden. In the distance tiny lights flicker. A cow moos somewhere. Maybe I can stay at home tomorrow. I cud lie in bed in the mornen and pretend I'm too tired. Mammy might believe me.

Daddy an James check the bags every day. When they see brown stains or damp spots they lift the bag an dump it onto the skip. They throw away the stained bag an bad potatoes. They put the good wans into a new bag an sew it up agen.

Wan day when I arrive home from school a black van is parked outside the barn. A man talks to Daddy. It must be the inspector. I stand by the door. The inspector waalks along the row. He reaches up an tugs some bags. He pokes others. He waalks back. He stoops. He sniffs. He lucks up to the tap row. 'Can you get this one down?' Daddy opens the bag. The inspector cuts the string an pushes the bag over. Potatoes roll over the cement. He steps round them picken up a sample. He rubs them. He sniffs them. He puts the potatoes back in the bag. 'I'd like to check the weight.' Daddy places the bag on the weighbridge. The fifty-six pounds weights rise and fall, rise an fall agen. It settles. 'That's all fine. We'll have them all.'

Pythagoras

We line up outside the classroom door. His muffled voice echoes through it. We ken't make out what he's sayen. We stand in silence. Chairs scrape on the classroom floor. The door swings open and he waalks out with his soutane swayen over his black shinen shoes. He ignores us. Their tips pop in an out with each step. The laces flap. The heels clatter. His eyes stare. They're red agen. He rubs his hand through his blond hair an flattens it down. In the other hand he holds a packet of Players an a silver lighter. He takes a cigarette out, taps it on the box an lets it droop from his lips. The lighter clicks. He breathes in an moves outside. He strolls up an down the gravel path kicken pebbles. He taps the half-smoked cigarette between his thumb an finger. The stub of ash falls down his front.

When the other class has left we enter without speaken. The chairs grate agen. The buckles a bags clatter on the desks. Coughs an splutters clear our throats. I sit on the second seat from the back in the left row. The outside door slams. 'It's Johnnie,' somebody whispers usen Father Gallagher's nickname.

I freeze. I squeeze me fingers into me palms so hard me knuckles go white. I stare at the Pythagoras theorem in me exercise book: *a squared plus b squared equals c squared. In a right-angled triangle the square of the hypotenuse is equal to the sum of squares of the other two sides*. I repeat it over an over. I don't understand. He swaggers to the blackboard. He struts to an fro. His eyes rove from side to side, looken for somewan to be his first victim.

He'll choose me or Kevin, Hugh or Neil from Carndonagh. He'll want to play to the Moville and Buncrana boys. They'll laugh at his sarcastic comments because they'll be too scared not to. He picks up the duster an wipes aff a venn diagram. 'Well, good old Pythagaros today, isn't it?' Waven the duster above his head.

Nobody speaks. I stare at me page. He staps. I wait. We all wait. A cough disturbs the silence. Please don't esk me. Bang! The duster thumps the cupboard beside me. I flinch. 'That's woken you up, O'Doherty, hasn't it? P for Pythagoras and P for Patrick. How about that?'

I think of the camogie stick lyen in the storeroom behind the cupboard doors. They lead to a passageway under the classrooms upstairs. Thick string tied tight round the knobs keep the doors shut. It tells me he's not used 'Excalibur' for a while. He mustn't be drinken as much. 'The blackboard's all yours, O'Doherty.'

I glance at me exercise book. I walk to the blackboard. I feel eyes staren at me. I cough. I pick up a piece a white chalk. It laves its hollow shape in the white dust on the ledge with the bare wood peepen through. I stare at the blackboard covered in a layer a dust. Father Gallagher lies back in his chair by the wall, tappen his fingers on Donal's desk.

'Th, th, th, the square a the hypotenuse is equal to the sum a the squares on the other two sides,'

'We could be here all day,' Father Gallagher sighs to Donal. 'So what does that mean?'

'It, it, it means that when ye hev a triangle with a ri, ri right angle an ye add a square to the sides, the b, b, b big square will hev the same area as the other square, Father.'

'Show me.'

My hands shake. I draw a square. The lines will not go straight. I stare at it, urgen me memory to help me.

'What's that supposed to be?'

'A square, Father.'

'That must be a Malin Head square,' he sniggers. The class giggles. I rub out the diagram an start agen. The lines are clearer an straighter. I add a triangle to the tap. 'Is that meant to be a right-angled triangle?'

'Yes, Father.'

'Carry on,' he says smiling at everyone. I add the last two squares an stand away from the blackboard.

'I never knew the squares were supposed to be the same size.'

'They're not, Father.'

'This is going to be fun. Carry on.'

'C, c, c is the longest side. A an B are the other two sides. Th, th, th the square corner is ninety degrees. The two small squares are the same area as the big one. Th, th, the formula is a squared plus b squared equals c squared Father.'

'Johnnie' strolls towards the cupboard doors. He bends down. His backside sticks out. He steps backwards, swingen the camogie stick over his shoulder. He taps the flat end of the stick twice on the red line on the cement.

'Let's be having you.'

I place me toes against it. I bend over til me fingers touch me laces.

'This might teach you to learn Pythagoras properly.'

Grippen it with both hands, he swings it across his chest. It hits me backside so hard I lunge forward.

'One. Get back here,' gritten his teeth.

'Two.'

83

A tear drops near me toes. I want to scream but don't. I mustn't show the others I'm a softie. I don't cry. Maybe I shud. I want to grab the camogie stick an force him to bend over. I want to beat him so hard he'll bleed. I want to see his blood on the floor.

'I told you not to move. Three.'

I fall forward. Two tears faal.

'You do that again and I'll give you double. Four.'

I tense me body. I screw up me face an eyes. Tears trickle down the side of me nose.

'Five.' I tense me toes an dig them into me shoes.

'Six. Learn it properly for tomorrow.'

I don't reply.

'I said learn it properly for tomorrow.'

'Yes, Father.'

He stands Excalibur in the corner. Silence. I whimper. I shuffle back to me seat. I slide to and fro to aise the stingen. A warm damp seeps through the backside a me trousers. It goes cold. The back a me knee is wet. The patch grows bigger round me thighs. It blackens me grey trousers. I cross me legs an pull the tail a me coat over them.

'For God's sake, Donal, come up here and do it properly for the amadans at the back.' Donal smiles an waalks to the blackboard. When he's finished Father Gallagher claps. He clears his throat, sighs an pushes himself aff the chair.

'Excalibur, my dear Excalibur,' he says picken up the camogie stick. He haulds it out from his chest. His hand begins to shake. He breathes heavily. He takes a step forward exclaimen: *'Is this a dagger which I see before me, The handle toward my hand? Come, let me clutch thee. I have thee not, and yet I see thee still.'*

He strides across the front a the classroom staren at the stick. A tear runs down his cheek. His voice trembles. He staps an stares at the ceilen. He kerries on. He staps agen an stares at us. His eyes bulge. He swings the stick above his head an bangs it on his desk. We jump. He laughs.

Ploughing

'Ye wait here this time an build that load a tirf,' Daddy says.

As soon as they had finished the tea an sandwiches Mammy made, Robbie, Dennis, me brother James an Daddy set aff to Glentogher for another load with the long trailer an blue Fordson Major tractor. I head to the load of tirf scattered on the gravel behind the barn. I pick out the longest pieces and lay them side by side in a straight line. I kerry on til I've made a rectangle the same size as the other stack. With each new row, I move the tirf in a little so the sides slant to allow the rain to drain aff. After three rows I fork the small tirf into the centre of the rectangle with a tirf graip. I stand at the end an luck along the rows. If there are any bulges I hit them with the graip. I pile some behind the long ones to stop them fallen inwards. As the rows reach head height I lay a ladder against them and tap them aal the way along to make the side flat. I throw up armfuls of long tirf. I don't use the graip because it breaks them. Their hard, jagged surface scrapes me face an arms. I climb the ladder an add them to the rows. I move the ladder along. As the sides get higher the centre gets smaller an smaller. Dust flies in me face as I fork the clods up. At the tap I lay wan row of long tirf side by side to stap rain seepen in. I gather the tiny pieces lyen on the ground into creels.

They won't be back for at least an hour an a half I think to meself. I waalk to the end of the street at the front of the house. I luck across the fiels towards the road. I ken't see or hear the tractor. I sit on the red Massey Ferguson tractor parked by the gate into the grass fiel. The plough, attached to the back, rests on the gravel to stap the tractor from moven. Orange baler twine sways from the ignition key. The fiel of grass sways this way an that. James must be ploughen later. I luck agen for the blue Fordson Major. I listen. Silence. I open the gate. I climb onto the Massey Ferguson, pull the gear stick back halfway to neutral an tirn the key. Blue smoke wafts over me head as the engine splutters. It staps. I try agen. More blue smoke belches out. I pull the throttle back. The engine roars. Black smoke starts to pump out. I slide up the hydraulic lever for the plough. It jolts up. The tractor shakes. I luck towards the kitchen door.

I steer into the fiel an stap at the side near the rodeen. I slide down the hydraulic lever. The plough rests on the ground. With the tractor in first gear, I set aff. I luck behind an lower the lever until the plough is at the right depth. If it's not deep enough the soil won't turn. If it's too deep the tractor won't be able to pull. I head down the side of the field keepen as close as I ken to the rodeen. The plough cuts through the grass an curls the black shiny soil over. It crumbles. Worms fall out. The grass disappears. Seagulls hover an squawk. At the end of the fiel I turn right an kerry on along the bottom, turn right along the barbed wire an turn right agen to head back to the gate. I luck at the furrow all the way round the edge of the fiel.

I start ploughen another furrow. I kerry on. As I get nearer the middle of the fiel the furrows become shorter an shorter, laven little space to turn. I raise the plough an drive over the ploughed soil. The narrow front tyres disappear. The rear wheels spin. They lave a wide deep track. They flatten the clay. The tractor groans. When I arrive at the gate two parallel channels stretch behind me across a spiral of furrows. Hollows the size of me fist show where the rubber grips dug deeper.

Mammy waves. I smile. I drive the tractor out the gate onto the gravel. Lumps of clay fall aff the rear wheels. I ease the throttle an pull the gearstick into neutral. She shouts somethen. I turn aff the engine.

'What in God's name are you doing?'

'I thought I'd plough for Daddy. The tractor an plough were here so I just did it.'

'Who told you?'

'Nobody.'

'Jesus, Mary and Joseph, the good field of grass!'

I hear the tractor. It must be them. I luck towards the hill at Mullen's. Black smoke rises above the bushes as the Fordson Major climbs the hill. It passes the chapel. Two men sit on tap. It must be the neighbours Robbie and Dennis. The tractor tirns at The Square Toe corner. It passes Mary Anne's shop. It slows down as it tirns into our lane. Robbie waves. I wave back. Dennis shouts somethen but I ken't make out what he says. James reverses the trailer alongside the stack. He lucks at the fiel I've ploughed. He laughs an waalks away.

'That's a grand job y'eve done there, Patrick,' Robbie calls.

Daddy steps down from the back seat and looks at the tirf stack.

'Pretty good,' he nods.

He lucks at the fiel and my spiral furrows. He scratches his head. He throws his arms in the air. He tirns and stares at me. I run.

Veni, vidi...

I repeat over an over the Imperfect Tense of the first, second an third conjugations for Father O'Reilly. It's hard to remember them with all the laughen an talken: portabam, portabas, portabat, portabamus, portabatis, portabant. Monebam, monebas, monebat, monebamus, monebatis, monebant. Capiebam, capiebas, cabiebat, capiebamus, capiebatis, capiebant.

    The bus slows down as it climbs Chapel Street an stops outside Mariner's Shop. The boys an girls goen to The Tech push an shove along the aisle. They yank each other's bags. They tease wan another about who fancies who. I sit an wait. I stare at the shop. The door is shut. It's dark inside. The white ice cream machine with its silver lever for maken cones is covered with a red towel. I want wan of Dick Mariner's curly wurley 99's with strawberry sauce. I'll hev to wait til a quarter to four. Danny Tulley presses a button near the steeren wheel. The bus door hisses lake a punctured tractor tyre. It folds back against the rail. 'Stop shuven, will ye,' he shouts.

    The clock on the spire of The Sacred Heart Cathedral bongs nine o'clock. Father O'Reilly will be starten the Latin Lesson. I recite me verbs agen. I try to remember the other verbs he mentioned yesterday but I ken't. Everybody clambers aff and disappears round the corner at Church Street. Their voices and laughter fade. I step aff sayen goodbye to the girls waiten to travel to the convent. 'Bloody hell, they're a rowdy lot, that Tech crowd. They gi'me a fecken headache ivry mornen an evenen. Ye behave yirself for them priests,' Danny grumbles as the door swishes shut.

    I smile an wave to the girls as the bus sets aff. I cross over to Pound Street, reciten the regular verbs. I can't remember the others. Across the street the boys' an girls' heads move along the inside of the Tech playground wall as they line up. Yes! It's amo, moneo and capio. The Future Tense. Amabo, amabis, amabit, amabimus, amabitis, amabunt. Monebo, monebis, monebit, monebimus, minebetis, minebunt. Capiam, capies, capiet, capiemus, capietis, capient. I rush down Pound Street. I pass McCarroll's Vets an McLaughlin Builders. I think of what Mammy told me about them builden our house when I was wan year old. She taalked about Big Jim, the boss.

    Father O'Reilly's silver Ford Zephyr with its silver grille is parked opposite the metal gate with tall vertical rods. I want to kick the car. I grab wan rod an push. My fingers go cold. The cracked rust sticks to me skin. I flick it away. The gate squeaks. The bottom bar drags on the cement step. I shut the gate. The latch clicks.

It's five past nine on the Cathedral clock. I tiptoe over the gravel half buried in weeds to the cement footpath. I crouch. I don't know why I crouch because I ken't reach the bottom of the tall windows. I stop an luck up. A long rope dangles from the tap of the frame. It sways. He always esks John Sweeney to pull it to open the small window. I listen but I ken't hear anythen. I climb the four stone steps. I push the black metal knob as big as my fist. The heavy wooden door swings inwards on its two black metal hinges bolted halfway across. I grab the knob to stop the inside latch bangen into the hole it's made in the plaster. I step towards the classroom door.

Father O'Reilly is taalken but I ken't make out what he's sayen. He sounds calm. He mustn't be in a bad mood. I luck through the keyhole. He's standen at the front. The black buttons on his stomach shine. His fat hand covers the duster. My seat is empty. There's a line of writen on the blackboard. I ken't read it. I brush me ear against the lock. 'Well, boys, it's The Imperfect and The Future, isn't it?' Silence.

'Is anyone awake? Silence.
'For God sake, Donal, say something, will you.'
'Yes, Father.'

The future. Please don't esk me about the future. I want to stay here. Maybe I'll hide in the toilets. I'll sneak into Geography afterwards. Somebody will tell on me. If only the bus had broken down. He wudn't believe me. He'd accuse me of tellen lies. I knock an enter. I shut the door. I sit down quickly. 'Ah, ah, look who's here. Well, O'Doherty, you didn't rush yourself. Just in time for our verb test.'

I wish he'd stop callen me O'Doherty. My name is Doherty. I don't know why he calls me O'Doherty. The boys from Buncrana and Moville laugh when he calls me O'Doherty. I don't care what they think. I beat them at Latin and French. They don't taalk to me unless they need help. I don't esk them to help me with Maths.

At lunchtime they crowd round Mike, the All-Ireland Irish dancing champion. He's so skinny he hops, skips, jumps, an flings his feet in the air lake a bird. Frank copies him. He stops after a couple of steps. His legs are too long. The others try. They faal over an laugh. When Dinny McLaughlin, the retired Irish Dancing Champion, comes into school he esks Mike to teach us. He struts in front of us, showen aff. He stops and expects us to do the same. I'm a culchie. A loner. A poor farmer's son with big hands an long steps. A thick boy who shudn't be at The College. I'll only iver be a farmer. I'm just a waste of teachers' time. I put me bag on the floor. I slide into me half of the double desk second from the front beside Kevin. I take out me jotter, textbook an pen.

Father O'Reilly stands by the tall rotaten blackboard, tappen the duster on the wooden frame, the other hand buried in his soutane pocket. He doesn't speak. I open me books. I hauld me pen. I stare at the pages. 'Seeing you've kept us waiting, O'Doherty, perhaps you can tell us what we did yesterday,' steppen towards me an tapping my desk.

I stare at the blackboard. 'Hmmm. Regular verbs, Father.'

'What about them?' raisen the duster above his shoulder.

'Hmmm. The Imperfect and The Future.'

'What about them?' his voice becomen deeper an louder. He screws up his face an rubs his fingers through his thick, black, curly hair.

'We lucked at regular verbs, Father.'

'And?' His knuckles goen white.

'The first, second, an third conjugations, Father.'

'And?'

'The Imperfect an Future, Father.'

'Give me the Imperfect first person plural of vocare.'

Vocare, vocare, vocare. Yes. First declination. Vocabam, vocabas, vocabat, vocabamus, vacates, vacabant. Yes, it must be vocabamus.

'Hurry up, O'Doherty,'

'Vocabamus, Father.'

'Not bad, O'Doherty.'

He steps towards the blackboard. His shinen black shoes pop out with ivry stride. He catches the metal strip an slides it up. He swipes the duster back an forth. He blows the dust away. I take a deep breath an sigh. I smile at Kevin. He smiles back.

'The Future. Let's see,' tappen the duster on the front desk. I wait for him to push a piece of chalk into me chest. He turns towards Hugh. 'Well, Hugh, how would you do it?' Given him the chalk. Hugh begins to write. Monebo, monebis, monebit, monebamus, monebitis, monebunt. His hand shakes. 'Say it as you write it,' His voice quivers. He turns round. His eyes are red. 'Finished?' Father O'Reilly calls from the back of the room.

'Yes, Father,' wipen his eyes.

'Anyone got anything to say about that?' He stops behind me. He pushes the duster into me shoulder. I cringe. 'He's got wan wrong, Father,' looken straight ahead.

'I hope you're right. Or else.' My hands shake. I check Fr. O'Reilly's list. I check Hugh's list. 'First person plural, Father.' My voice quiveren.

'Well?'
'He's put an 'a' instead of an 'i', Father.'
'So what's the whole spelling then?'
'Monebimus, Father.'
'Well, what do you think, Hugh?'
'Yes, he's right, Father.'
'So you mean you're wrong?'
'Yes, Father.'
'Well, you know what to do for tomorrow, don't you?'
'Yes, Father.'

Hugh's niver cried before. He's niver made a mistake. I want to kick Father O'Reilly. I want him to feel the pain. He turns his wrist over to check his watch. Its leather strap sinks into his brown spotty fat skin. He flicks through the Latin textbook from Neil's desk. 'What page is it?
'Thirty-four, Father.'
'We went through all of this yesterday. I want everyone to study this again now in silence. You obviously don't know it.'

Father O'Reilly tucks his newspaper under his oxter. He searches in the deep pocket of his soutane an heads out the door. He leaves it half open. His cigarette lighter clicks. He splutters. The pages rustle. He comes back in. 'Tomorrow I'll test the whole class on the Imperfect and Future again and we'll do some translation,' sliden the strap into his pocket. 'For your homework write out ten First Conjunction verbs, five Imperfect and five Future.'

With the newspaper sticken out of his pocket he heads towards the door, his shoes clumpen on the wooden floor. The door slams. While we wait for Mr. McKennagh to come in for Geography we talk quietly without laven our seats. I nudge Hugh sitten in front of me. His back shivers. His hands cover his face. He turns. 'Listen, there's a quick way to do yer lines. I did it for Campbell. He didn't notice.' Hugh tries to smile.

Turf

Me bedroom door opens. 'Need ye to come to Glentogher,' Daddy says.

Yes! Saved from Father Campbell. He hates me. I don't lake history. He uses the strap when I get it wrong. Mammy doesn't lake me missen school because she doesn't want me to end up lake the other boys hangen round home and getten the dole.

I pull on a blue sweater that came in a parcel from Auntie Ellen in New York. The camphor makes me snort. I don't mind wearen the clothes she sends. I slip on a pair of grey socks that Mammy knitted. They're soft an fluffy. Mammy's in the scullery. She stands plates in the wicker basket. She puts a bottle of fresh milk wrapped in a tea towel in the corner. She covers two wheaten scones in another tea towel, rolls six eggs in pieces of *The Derry Journal* an places them between the scones an the plates. She puts a block of butter wrapped in tinfoil between a pot of blackberry an apple jam an a jam jar of tealeaves. She rolls the knives, forks an spoons in another towel an slides them between the jars. 'A day in Glentogher, hey? Make sure you have gaiters. The bog'll be soaking after last night's rain.'

I gulp me cornflakes, two slices of wheaten bread with butter an jam. I slurp me cup of tea. I push me feet into me boots by the back door. I push hard to bend the leather. I pull the leather laces. They rub through the eyes. 'Here, take this to the trailer. You'll need to hurry up. They're ready to go.'

I grab the gaiters made from the taps of auld wellingtons. I pick up the basket. The twigs are smooth. They've hardened. They're not soft anymore lake the wans Daddy cuts aff the sally rod tree down by the salmon hole to whip me legs. It's a quarter past eight. Roger Tamm, Robbie Merchant an Daddy nail sheets of wood on three sides of the trailer. He throws in two bags of straw to sit on, chains to pull out the tractor if it bogs, raincoats, forks an two tirf spades.

'Ye'll hev te drive the Ford Dexta. James's gone ahead with the Massey Ferguson.' I lake driven the Ford Dexta. It's fast an the gears change without any trouble. I think of the black smoke pumpen out a the exhaust an blowen over me head when I cart slat mara on the trailer from the shore to put on the potato field. Daddy won't esk Roger or Michael because they don't hev tractors. I ken't remember where me provisional licence is. I hope the garda don't stap me in Carndonagh. I turn away an smile. I grip me hands with joy but turn back quickly.

Everybody scrambles into the trailer. They make themselves comfortable on the bags of straw an rest their backs against the wooden sheets. They wrap the auld coats round their legs. 'Right, aff we go,' a voice calls.

'Full steam ahead now, Patrick,' Roger laughs.

'Nah, ye won't,' Daddy frowns.

I puff up the seat for the fifteen miles drive to Glentogher. I turn the key. The tractor jumps forward. 'For Christ's sake. Yer maken a right hames a it,' Daddy bellows. I don't reply. I wait for him to jump aff the trailer. I put the tractor into neutral. I check it. I check it agen. 'What's keepen ye? I turn the key agen. The engine splutters. A cloud of blue smoke shoots from the exhaust.

'Yippee,' shouts Roger.

'Hope ye've linked up the trailer,' Robbie jokes, a cigarette hangen from his mouth.

I push the clutch with me left foot, flick the brake lever with me right an grind the gearstick forward into first gear. I pull the throttle back a little an aise me fut aff the clutch. I hope the engine doesn't stap. If it does the trailer will jolt. Daddy'll shout. He might throw somethen, jump down an pull me aff. He'll hit me across the head. I grip the steeren wheel. The hum of the engine changes. It sounds lake it's goen to stap. The tractor moves. The trailer squeaks. The wheels bounce over the gravel. I luck round. Everyone's head bounces. Streaks of grey hair flap up an down. Daddy sits near the edge, Robbie in the middle an Roger at the end. They chatter but I ken't hear what they're sayen.

I pull the throttle back a bit more an change into second gear as I climb the brae in Carn Malin. I pass Mary Anne's shop. The door's shut. A bulb shines in the kitchen. Big Dennis' house is closed. It's dark inside. I slow down at Michael Paddy Brian's house on the sharp bend. He stands at the front door a his white cottage. His black an white sheepdog barks. He waves. I wave back. Daddy believes he stands there all the time watchen our house because he arrives on his bicycle whenever he sees us worken outside. Daddy never tells him anythen because he knows Michael will tell ivrybody. He's niver laked Michael since he built a stone wall on the corner to stap drivers flattenen his grass verge.

I edge out onto the main road at The Square Toe. I don't know why it's called The Square Toe. It's shaped lake a T. There's nothen square about it. It's nothen lake a toe. I must esk Michael. Ivrybody says he knows ivrythen. I work me way up through the gears to third. I pull the throttle back as far as it'll go. The tractor hurtles over the rough tarmac on the brae outside the chapel. We all make a quick sign of the cross. Me ears flap. Me cheeks shiver. I close me mouth to stap me teeth chatteren. Me hair flies backwards. Me eyelids flicker. The mist covers the tap of The Black Mountain in the distance. I'll hev to change gear. The tractor'll stap an run back. I pull the throttle agen as I approach the bottom a the hill. The tractor speeds up but begins to slow down. I need to do ivrythen at the right time. I think back to seein' James doen it so quickly. I ease the throttle, press the clutch, pull the gear lever back to the left, take me foot aff the clutch an pull the throttle at the same time. 'Done it.'

'Hurray,' the men shout to each other.

It's half past eight. At the tap of The Black Mountain I aise the throttle an press the brake slowly. I luck across to The Five Fingers Strand and Trawbreaga Bay where ships were sunk duren the world wars. The little white houses on The Isle of Dough stand out lake white dots on the far side a the bay. There's a famine village there. Mr. O'Leary taught us about The Great Famine in 1845. He said the English caused it because they wudn't feed anywan.

The hill down is steep an twisted. I put the tractor into first gear. It groans its way to the bottom. I keep me fut on the brake. The engine groans lake a cow calven. The road flattens an widens. I pull the throttle back an speed towards Malin Town. I pass Father McGoldrick's three storey cream presbytery surrounded by fir trees. I remember him shouten at me at school when I was preparen for Confirmation. I slow down as I drive past the triangular green and the rows of flowerbeds an window boxes in 'Ireland's tidiest town' of Malin, a plantation town. Cuhoon's petrol station is open. They're Protestants. Bogg's butchers is open. They're Protestants too. I niver know when the shops are open here. I speed up as I cross the bridge out a the town.

It's a quarter to nine. Three miles ahead the spire a The Sacred Heart Cathedral disappears into the clouds hangen over Carndonagh. My fingers are numb from holden the steeren wheel. I remove wan hand an wiggle them an then the other hand. I straighten an bend me leg, then the other. I wriggle me backside sunk into the bag of straw. James laves home at six o' clock on Mondays to drive two loads of cattle for neighbours to the market in Carndonagh. He has to drive slowly.

I slow down along Church Street, pass The Diamond in the centre an along Chapel Street. McCarroll Vets is open. I stare at the garda station. A garda car is parked outside. The lights are on. I ken't see anywan. McLaughlin Builders is open. Mammy told me that Big Jim had seven brothers lake me. He taalked to me when Mammy asked me to get paint on the way home from school. I put a hand over me face as I pass The College. If Father O'Reilly spots me I'll be able to tell him tomorrow that I was cutten tirf in Glentogher. He'll tell me aff but at least I won't be in trouble when I get home.

I change down to first gear on the steep climb from the main road up to Glentogher. The sun is beginnen to shine. It glistens through the trees. I shade me eyes with wan hand. I grip the wheel tighter with the other. Sheep eat the scutch grass on the sides a the road. They stop an stare afore setten aff at full speed with their muck covered tails waggen. Their lambs, a little cleaner, scuttle along behind. It's twenty past nine. I stap at last year's clump of clods on the rodeen.

The mist, hiden the tap half of Slieve Snacht has nearly gone. The sun is getten warmer. 'Ye get the fire goen,' Daddy orders, climben down from the trailer. Roger an Robbie groan as they step down an straighten their backs.

Daddy heads aff down the family bink. I kerry the basket to the circle a stones blackened from last year's fire. I gather an armful a brown hairy tirf from the stack, screw up pages a *The Derry Journal* an put tirf on them. I sprinkle diesel from the bottle buried under the stones an strike a match. It dies out. I strike another. It lights, almost dies an lights up again. The paper blackens. It curls. The edges glow red. It turns grey an crumbles. The thin roots in the clods do the same. Yellow flames lick the clods. The flames grow wider. They climb higher. They change to orange. Their tips go red. Smoke rises. The bottom a them tirns a pale yellow. I fan the fire with a cloth from Mammy's basket. I pile small pieces a black tirf on tap.

I head down the bink. Nobody speaks. With a firm grip on the spade, Daddy shaves aff the wrinkled vertical face. Pieces fall into the brown water. He steps back an does the same agen all the way to the end. The wet surface shines. The tap is brown, hairy an spongey with heather roots. The middle is dark with thin orange roots. The bottom is black. There are no roots here. James, cutten through the heather, marks out a strip two feet wide all the way to the end. Kevin stands in the water an pushes his spade in sideways to slice the tap layer a sods. Robbie stands on the fresh soft surface. He leans on the sheep's horn handle an pushes his right-handed tirf spade down a futt deep. He eases the handle towards his stomach, lifts the tirf an lets it slip onto the heather. I stab it with a two-pronged fork an lay it further back. Robbie digs non-stop rubben his cap back an forth. I fork non-stop. Soon the heather is lake a tiled floor with row upon row of brown an black soggy turf.

It's twenty to eleven. In the distance a sheep baas. Its lambs baa. I luck round but ken't see them. At the roadside three black faced sheep with curlen horns pull at the grass at the edges of the tirf stacks. They swing their tails in the heat. Bits of fleece dangle from their stomach. An engine hums somewhere in the mist on the tap of Slieve Snacht. I kerry on stabben the tirf. I glance agen at the mountain. The hum increases. A white van appears. The hum gets louder as it descends. 'Ice cream van,' shouts Kevin, runnen as fast as he ken. 'Stap. Stap.'

The van slows down an staps. Kevin kerries a block of ice cream to Mammy's basket. He waalks up to us with plates an spoons. 'Good on ye,' says Robbie moven his cap back an forward agen. We stand an eat the vanilla chunks without speaken. The spoons scrape the plates. It's twelve o'clock.

'Ken ye put some more tirf on the fire an' boil them eggs. Make sure it's black tirf,' Daddy shouts to me.

'Go on ahead, Patrick,' Robbie says. 'I'll fork them tirf back for ye.'

The fire crumbles under the weight of the large teapot. Sparks spit out. I put the small saucepan on the flat burnen cinders. The yellow an red flames curl round it. I wait. I watch Daddy benden, twisten, throwen, an rubben the sweat away. Spots of tar on the road glisten. A sheep waalks past on its way to find more grass. Steam begins to spout from the tin teapot. The flames flicker. The fire hisses. An empty eggshell, chopped in two, sticks out from last year's soggy ash. I rub the smaller piece clean first an match the pieces as best I can. It's a quarter past twelve. I scoop out a fistful of soggy tirf from the edge of the bink an slide it into the divided eggshell. I stick the smaller slice on tap. I spit an rub it. A dirty jagged line goes all the way round. I rub it agen but it doesn't move. The water in the egg saucepan begins to simmer. I unwrap Mammy's eggs an slide them in. The grey stains on the eggshell dry in the sun. The jagged line lucks thinner. I lift it. It's solid. 'Is the water for the tae ready yit?' Daddy shouts.

'Nearly.'

An egg pops. A white thread of yoke wriggles to the surface. It changes to foam. The foam expands. It bubbles higher. I spoon it aff. The dirty white scum sticks to the sides an bubbles. The egg floats to the surface. I place the auld eggshell on a spoon an lower it into the saucepan. The water turns black. Bits a tirf float to the surface. The water boils agen. The teapot hisses. I add two heaped spoons of tealeaves an lave it on the side. I guess how long to wait for the eggs. I drain them. 'Right. Ready,' I shout.

Daddy sticks his spade into the heather. He heads towards me. The others follow. They shuffle round the fire. Daddy wipes his forehead. He haulds out his hand, staren at the ground. I hand round the eggs. I keep the false wan to wan side. I hand it to Roger maken sure the muddy crack is at the bottom. He strikes it with a knife. The tap flies into the fire. A thick black gunge oozes down the side an over his fingers. He freezes. He stares at the egg. He stares at me. The white a his eyes grow larger. He lucks at the blade. Ivrybody staps an stares. Nobody speaks. His eyes narrow. He bends towards me, stretchen his neck. 'Wh,wh, wh, wh, what the fuck is this?'

The knife sticks up from his white knuckled fist. Daddy jerks his head towards me. He stares but doesn't know what to do. I wait for him to dive. He lowers his head an scrapes the bottom of his eggshell. He scrunches it. He throws it over his shoulder. He lucks at Roger. James taps his shoe with his spoon. He lucks at me, tryen not to laugh. He gets up an heads back to the tirf. Kevin buries his chin in his chest. His shoulders shake. He lucks away an heads after James. Roger, his face reddenen, lunges towards me, flailen his arms an legs. Ash scatters. I jump backwards, splutter an blow. He throws the egg at me. I duck. 'Co, co, co, come here, ye little fu, fu, fu, fucker,' spittle landen on me face. I scramble to me feet. 'Me fucken' teeth, where are they?' Roger turns onto his hands an knees afore standen up. He slaps the dust aff his trousers an runs towards me. 'Ye little fu, fu, fu, fucker,' pushen the knife nearer. I run as fast as I ken, glancen behind. Roger gropes in the ashes. Dust scatters. Daddy gets up an waalks back to his spade.'Me fucken te, te, teeth. Where are ye, ye bastard?'

James, Kevin an Robbie bend over their spades laughen. I'll get ye, ye little cunt.' By the time Roger finds his teeth I'm at the far end a the road. I crouch in the long heather. He kicks the fire an marches down to James an Kevin. He shouts but I ken't make out what he's sayen. He waves his hands about in the air. They laugh.

'Get back here,' Daddy shouts waven his fist in the air. He'll batter me. I waalk back watchen him an Roger. They kerry on cutten tirf. Nobody speaks. I waalk to James. I pick up the graip. I stab the tirf an place them beside the others. I keep my head down an pretend not to luck at Roger. He grunts an stomps round with his graip, droppen the tirf anywhere. He'll throw it at me. I rub the sweat from me head. My collar sticks. I rub me neck. It stings from the sun. Mammy told me to put a hat on. I don't want to wear a hat. I'll luck silly. Nobody else wears a hat. Daddy lucks stupid with an auld knotted hankerchief on his head.

We work all afternoon, cutten, forken, benden an wipen the sweat from our foreheads an necks. At three o'clock the sun goes down behind Slieve Sneacht. Two more hours an I'll be driven the tractor home. Maybe Daddy won't let me. I don't want to sit in the trailer with Roger. 'It's half past four. We'll lave the next bit till the morra,' Daddy says to ivrywan without lucken at me.

We pack up. Roger steps into the trailer. He doesn't speak. Daddy an Michael follow. It lucks lake I'll be driven. Daddy might've calmed down by the time we get home. I cud tell Mammy. She'd find it funny.

When we arrive home Mammy is outside the henhouse scatteren a tin a corn on the gravel. 'How ye, Lizzie,' says Michael steppen down with his spade over his shoulder.

'You've finished early?'

'Aye, just finished wan lot. Bin a good day though with a lot of laughs. Roger lost his teeth.'

'How'd that happen?'

Ah, now then. That'd be tellen. Ye'll hev to esk Patrick.

I stare at Michael. Daddy waalks into the barn. He'll be cleanen his spade with the same auld cloth dipped in engine oil. He'll hang the spade on the metal prong near the hay rake. I waalk towards the house. He follows. I go to the bathroom. Dishes rattle in the kitchen. 'Dinner's ready,' Mammy calls. I sit opposite Daddy.

'So what's this about Roger?' she esks.

I luck at Daddy. He lucks at his plate. He doesn't speak.

The Troubles

A man waved his torch towards lane twelve. I sat in the arrival lounge, sipping coffee from a cardboard cup. I tried to write again.

I embarked and headed to the quiet zone. Through the glass doors I saw people watching TV. It was reporting on the aftermath of the I.R.A's bomb that exploded in Belfast the week before injuring twenty people and damaging seven hundred houses. John Major was speaking.

Algebra

It's Thursday morning. I hate Thursday mornings. I think a little else. We sit, all thirty a us, in single benches arranged in three rows a ten desks from nine o'clock waiten for the casual clump a Father Campbell's shinen leather shoes on the bare wooden floor a the corridor outside our classroom. Silence. He enters from the back a the classroom. It's 9.15. I dare not luck round. His long black soutane swishes round his legs in tune with his waddlen frame as he taps each boy nearest him on the head with the rolled up daily *Independent* on his way to the shinen brown desk at the front. Threads a pipe smoke waft over his shoulder. He's playen with us. I cower as soon as I hear the flick a the newspaper approachen from behind. It doesn't hurt. He shuffles his chubby body onto the stool lake Mammy used to slide onto the chair when she was waitin with Brendan.

Every Thursday it's the same routine; he takes the 's' shaped pipe from between the few tar-stained teeth he has left, peers into the ash, hopen to find enough tobacco left for a smoke at playtime. He slides it down into the long deep pocket where the leather strap hides. He opens the newspaper, turns each page with his right hand while resten the left on his thigh. I wish a spark would fall out a the pipe, singe his pocket an burn his skin. For a moment, I imagine a thin layer a smoke swirlen round his trousers. I urge it to speed up. It's 9.20. Father Campbell shatters the silence when he splutters an wheezes. 'Well, what are we doing today?'

No-one speaks. 'I said what are we doing today?' Nobody speaks. He raises his eyes above his heavy black rimmed jam-jar glasses an surveys the sea a pale faces looken downwards. 'God, it's like talking to myself here.' Even though Frank is staren at his work, he senses that Father Campbell is waiten for him to say somethen. They luck at each other. 'You're about the only one who seems to be awake this morning, Frank. So what's the homework, then?'

Frank's hands began to shake. 'You asked us to do exercises A and B on page 54, Father,' his hands an voice tremblen.

'Oh. I think I'll let one or two of you show us how they should be done. What do you think, Frank?'

Frank replies with a nervous smile. Father Campbell's head, bald apart from a few long strands a hair flattened from left to right on the tap with Brylcreem, swings lake an owl with its bulgen eyes lucken for someone to attack. 'You. You'd like to. Wouldn't you?

I luck at him, hopen he has picked someone else. Everyone lucks at him, hopen he hasn't chosen them. Their eyes, full of pity, turn towards me. 'Yes. You. Can you not see I'm staring at you? That means you do the question. You'd better do it right. You remember what happened last week,' speaken through clenched teeth, his cheeks twitchen.

Me hands shake. I pick up me exercise book an head towards the blackboard behind him. He kerries on readen his newspaper. 'Leave it on your desk. You're not here to copy onto the board. Any fool can do that.'

Before I have time to return me book, he grabs it an throws it, not caren where it lands or who it hits. It's red cover flutters through the air an slides to the floor after hitten the wall. The square pattern pages, still stapled together, slide along the floor an come to a quick stop near someone's chair. I pick up a used stick of white chalk an begin to write. No matter how hard I try I ken't remember the question. The newspaper rustles. He clears his throat. If I tell him I've forgotten the question he'll take out his strap or punch me in my spine. If I say nothen he'll order me to write it fifty times for the morra. That means I'll have to buy a new exercise book. I don't have any money. I'll have to esk Mammy. I hope she doesn't tell Daddy.

'Have you fallen asleep?'

'No, Father.'

'Well, get on with it.'

'I ken't, Father.'

'What do you mean you can't?'

'I ken't remember the question, Father.'

'For God's sake, use your brain and get a book. Do I have to tell you everything?'

I go to Neil in the front desk, borrow his textbook an rush back to the blackboard. The chalk trembles in me raised hand. It squeaks as I attempt to write in large numbers. He tauld me aff before for writen too small. I press hard to make the numbers wan an five. Crack! The chalk snaps. A piece bounces along the floor an rolls under his stool. He looks round, squints a threatenen glance an returns to his newspaper. The piece in me hand is long enough to grip.

'Don't waste my time. Go away. Write it out fifty times for tomorrow.'

I lave the chalk on the blackboard ledge an return to me desk. I want to pick up me ripped exercise book but dare not. A droplet of sweat tricklen down me spine makes me shiver. The damp collar of me white shirt rubs me skin. I wiggle me finger inside the collar.

'Right, next,' he announces with a raised voice.

Kevin, a nervous boy who sits beside me, knows he'll be next because that's the way Father Campbell works. If you are good at Maths ye sit on the right and if ye're not ye sit on the left. I am always on the left. I'll niver have a chance to sit on the right. Some of the boys on the right are not that good. He lakes them because they're altar servers. I don't serve Mass. He doesn't lake me. I'm from Malin Head. I don't lake him either. In fact, I hate him. By the time Kevin finishes there are only five minutes left afore the end of the lesson. 'Well, Frank, how did he do?'

'His answer seems ok, Father.'

'Ok? What do you mean ok? It's either right or wrong, isn't it?'

'It's right but...'

'It's wrong,' Father Campbell interrupts.

'Yes, Father.'

'You'll make a fine teacher, won't you, Frank. It's a good job I'm a patient man.' He slides up his sleeve an lucks at his silver bracelet watch. 'What's on page 55?'

'Exercises C and D, Father.'

'There's your homework for tomorrow.' He closes his newspaper, slides aff the stool an fumbles in his pocket for his pipe. With a sneer aimed at Kevin, he heads out the door, settlen his pipe between his teeth. We sit in silence. Kevin stands still til he's sure he's gone.

Going Home

The captain welcomed everyone, predicted a calm crossing and punctual arrival in Larne. From the deck I could see the road meandered along the Drumfries and Galloway coastline towards Carnryan, separating the stony beach from the clusters of houses below sheep-strewn hills. I thought of my father and how he had travelled for farm work in Scotland in the 1950s-60s. How he went on the cattle boats every spring and autumn to send money home. How he laboured on potato farms. How he lived in bothies with other Irish labourers and how he cried on St. Patrick's Day while hanging his shirt on the washing line.

He used to disappear from home without speaking to any of us. Mammy would tell me sometime later that he'd taken the twelve thirty bus from The Square Toe to Derry, another bus to Belfast and then the cattle boat from Belfast to Heysham.

As the ferry approached Larne, the faint outline of County Antrim's coastal road wound northwards along the cliffs as far as I could see. My steering wheel shivered on the corrugated ramp overlapping the concrete. More orange-clad men, pointing the way ahead, lined the single track to the security checkpoint. Black uniformed men stood under the shelter, staring at me with guns ready. Two army jeeps camouflaged themselves between lorries. They let me through without stopping.

'Yes! yes!' I punched the air. Legacy fear lingered in my stomach. Guilt for nothing. I followed the blue and white M2/M22 signs for Derry along the A8 Larne – Milbrook – Ballynure.

A57 Ballyclare.

M2 Templepatrick.

M22 Antrim. Two Protestants killed because they had Catholic girlfriends.

Randalstown. A police officer killed by an IRA bomb.

A6 Moneynick.

Toome.

Castledawson. Where Seamus Heaney was born.

Curran

Knockcloghrim

Maghera. Fourteen people were murdered.

Dungiven. Seven murders.

Claudy. Nine murders. *Bloody Monday.*

Killaloo.

Ardmore.

A2 Derry. So many dead and injured.

102

So many.

At the junction of A2 and Spencer Road a man strolled along the red, white and blue kerbstones. A gable mural in the same colours read 'No Catholics here'. I waited for the traffic lights to change. I drove over The Foyle Bridge. The lights turned red. I followed the one-way system onto Bridge Street and turned right into John Street lined with its green, white and gold kerbstones. *Bloody Sunday* four streets away. Brian, from college, telling me that he never played cowboys and Indians. They only played Catholics and Protestants.

Cheating

It's the third lesson. I wish it was the first lesson. I want it out of the way. I sit on the back seat where Mr. O'Leary put me a few weeks ago because he said I was no good at History. I luck at the pages of notes in me jotter. I don't understand them. He'll ask me questions. I'll stutter. The boys from Buncrana an Moville will laugh at me. They'll call me *Froggie* agen because I sound lake a frog when I ken't get the words out.

I luck at the rollen blackboard with lines an lines of his handwriten from yesterday. His quick footsteps clatter along the corridor. I luck at the open door behind me. He pushes it hard. It bangs. He heads to the front of the class. His small case swings at his side. His long finger stretches over the gold-coloured lock. The leather patches on the elbows of his tweed jacket are cracked. The split up the back of his jacket curls at the bottom lake a pig's tail. The bottom of his black trousers dangle above his ankles. The heels of his black shoes are slanted. He slams the case on the desk an presses the lock. It springs back an hits the leather. Nobody speaks. He flicks the lid open. It bounces on the desk.

'Right, boys,' placen his folded leather strap on the table. 'Well, let's see what we were doing yesterday. Ah, yes, Louis XIV. France's longest serving king. The Sun King. The Franco-Dutch War and The Nine Year's War,' turnen towards his notes on the blackboard.

He surveys the class. Please don't esk me. I don't understand the wars, the battles, the armies or The Sun King. 'I can't see what you all find so funny,' he shouts as his red tie dangles from his open zip. 'I'll strap everyone of you if you don't stop,' bangen his strap on the table.

He picks up a long piece of chalk an starts to write below the silver metal strip that joins the sections a the blackboard. His fat wrist bends up an down as he squiggles. The lines slant as he reaches the edge of the blackboard. He pushes the metal bar. The blackboard moves up. His first few lines disappear over the top. He's written too fast. I ken't keep up. I've missed three lines. I screw up me face to make out what he's written next. I tilt me head wan way an then the other. I squint agen an agen. Me eyes hurt. I copy what I think he's written.

When I luck at the blackboard agen I ken't find the next words. I cover me writen with me other hand. I luck at Donal sitten next to me. I peep at his jotter. I ken't see what he's written. The backboard moves up agen. Yisterday's writen appears at the bottom. He kerries on. The old writen meets today's writen. He rubs out a few lines an kerries on. I make up words an sentences. I peep at Donal's book agen. I start a new paragraph to make it luck lake his. When he has filled the blackboard, he waalks back an forth across the front of the classroom with his hands behind his back. He lucks at the ceilen. He lucks at the floor. He frowns at us. He grumbles. He tirns towards the wall. He pushes his tie in an closes his zip. I kerry on writen. I shud wear the glasses Mammy got me, I'd see ivrythen. I don't want to wear them. Ivrybody'll laugh at me for sure. Mammy'll go mad if she finds out I don't wear them.

Me second year at the college Mr O'Leary teaches me History in a different classroom. He has the same case an strap. He wears the same trousers but shorter now. Wan of the leather patches on his jacket elbow is ripped. A leather button hangs loose on the front. The heel of his right shoe tilts outwards. The blackboard is wide an screwed to the wall. He writes lake last year. I can see it better because I'm in the third desk from the front. I copy his notes but they still don't make sense to me. I still hate History. I'll hide in the toilets. It's better when he dictates his notes to us. I can write what he says. I won't tell Mammy. She never esks about History. Daddy won't care. I hate Mr. O'Leary. I laugh to myself when I think of John from Buncrana. He was nicknamed John The General. One day afore Mr. O'Leary arrived in class John put a ball of black fluff on the blackboard ledge an attached a thread to it. He stuck a drawen pin in the other end of the ledge an unravelled the thread all the way back to his desk maken sure it lay flat on the floor along the wall. We sat. We waited for 'Yogi'. We sniggered.

'Yogi's comen,' shouted Neil peepen out the door.

Yogi came in an dropped his case on the desk. John tugged the thread. The fluff moved. 'Sir, a mouse!' The fluff moved. Yogi lucked round. He stared at me. He stared at the class.

'You think it's funny,' he bellowed. His eyes bulged. His cheeks wobbled. His chin reddened.

'Whose idea was this, then? Nobody spoke. He stared agen. 'For one minute, I'd cane the lot of you.' He thumped the strap into his case an slammed it shut. He marched out of the room. The door banged. We sniggered.

'He'll cane us all tomorrow. It's all your fault, John,' we muttered.

Day after day, week after week History is the same routine. Lines an lines of notes on the blackboard, copy them down an answer the questions. I hate the questions.

At the end of the year, I sit the History exam in the large hall above the classrooms. Three long rows of tables an chairs fill the hall. Mr. O'Leary strolls up an down between the rows, his hands clasped behind him. He rubs his thumb into the palm of his other hand. I stare at the questions. I luck round. I slide out the thin book I've hidden under me coat. I put it on me knees. I luck at the questions agen. I flick through the book. I luck round agen. I copy out a paragraph.

A week later he walks into the classroom with the exam papers under his arm. He hands them out. He calls out the marks. I wait. Mine is the last one. 'Patrick Doherty, zero.'

I stare. Me cheeks feel warm. I luck at me book. I don't reply. 'Well, Mr. Doherty, you've done an interesting paper, haven't you?'

I don't reply.

'Why did you cheat?'

'I didn't, Sir.'

'Out here now,' he says whippen the strap from his case. I waalk to the front of the class. 'I'll ask you again. Why did you copy?'

'But I didn't.' He lucks at the class an smiles. He raises the strap above his shoulder. I stretch out me hand.

'Don't pull away.'

The strap swishes across me palm. He lucks at me. His eyes bulge. The strap swishes agen. Its end wraps round me hand. It stings. It swishes agen. I pull me hand away. 'That's an extra one for pullen away. That'll teach you,' he says after six lashes.

I return to me seat an rub me palms between me legs.

'Serves you right, Froggie,' whispers Neil behind me.

The Sound of Music

It's eight o'clock. It's still dark. Mammy sits in the kitchen listenen to Radio Eireann. She's waiten to hear about what's happenen in The North, twenty miles away. 'It's going to rain. You need your duffle coat,' she says. There's no point in arguen. 'Button it up or you'll get cold standing at The Square Toe. Make sure you keep that hood up.'

I sneak past Mary Anne's shop. The curtains are still closed. I try to guess what sweets she'll give me when I call in on the way home. I hope it's not another gobstopper or piece of liquorice. The gobstopper's too gingery, an the liquorice sticks to me teeth. I might esk her for somethen different. I don't think Mammy or Daddy know she gives me sweets. I lake Aunty Mary Anne. She laughs an chats to me.

Michael Paddy Brian is mixen cement for the stone wall along the bend in the road outside his house. The council wants to straighten the bend because it's dangerous but he doesn't want to lose his land. Nobody'll help him. Daddy is angry because it's hard to drive the tractor an trailer round the corner without crossen to the other side. 'Aff to school agen, Patrick? A hear Paddy Kelly wuz hangen from the ladder on the back o the bus yesterday.'

'Aye. Hangen lake a drooked witterit, he wuz.'

'Ye wudn't do that, wud ye?'

'Na.'

Round the corner John Logue drags the tin forge door open over the gravel. He pushes a bag a coal against it. I take me coat aff, roll it into a ball and tuck it under me oxter. I luck at the upstairs windows of Iona House next to the bus stop. The curtains are open. I stare at them. I ken't see anywan. Patsy Rose Anne lives there sometimes. People come an stay but it's hard to tell when there's somebody there. If I see somebody I'll hide me coat under a whin bush. I tiptoe round the back. Two slanted wooden poles stick out of the garden with a rope stretched between them. A red an white towel wafts in the wind. I crouch under the kitchen window an listen. Silence. The back door is shut. I sneak past an reach up to the green wooden box on the wall. I don't know why it's there. The paint is peelen aff an the bottom hinge is broken. Chicken netten is nailed inside the door frame. I open it an wait for the squeak. It doesn't. The rain must've dampened it. I squash the coat inside an shut the door tight. The netten bulges. I sneak back to the bus stop. I luck back to the house. I still ken't see anywan. I've niver spoken to him. He has grey curly hair.

He wears glasses. The doors niver seem to open. I've niver seen any lights on.

The sleet stings me ears. I bend under a whin bush. I hold me leather bag on me head. I want to wear me duffle coat, but the others'll laugh at me. The Lough Swilly bus grinds up the hill past the coastguard station lake our Ford Dexta tractor. The red an yellow stripes along the side come into view when it tirns the corner. It speeds up on the straight flat road. The bus crawls to a stap. Its silver ladder curls over the roof from the back. I wonder how Paddy Kelly hung on to it. 'Mornen, Patrick,' says Danny. I smile an sit down.

'Mornen,' grunts Jim Doyle, the bus conductor, approachen from the back a the bus. I smile. He stares at me over the rim of his black rimmed glasses. He punches a hole in me monthly bus pass. 'A'll be watchen ye lads this afternoon. That clown down there cuda kilt himself yisterday if he fell aff that ladder on the back. Bloody amadan.'

He slides the hole punch back into the leather pouch at the side a his ticket machine. The machine dangles from its shoulder strap. It wobbles over his backside. He presses his hand against it to stap it hitten the seat as he puffs his way to the front seat. The bus staps at The Bree Inn. Eamonn an Declan waalk to the back a the bus without speaken to me.

I think about Derry. I've niver been there afore. I'll hev to make sure I don't get lost. I'll hev to get somethen to eat. Mammy says the people taalk funny in Derry. She doesn't lake the accent her sister, Catherine, has. I'm worried but I'm excited. I feel so good. A day on me own away from the priests an the Buncrana boys. They'll have Father Campbell for Maths an Science. Maybe I ken buy some sweets. When Mammy comes back from Derry she taalks about Littlewoods. I wonder if I ken find it. The bus arrives in Carn at ten to nine. Ivrywan gets aff apart from me an the girls goen to The Convent. 'Are ye not getten aff?' Esks Margaret, who's a year older than me.

'No,'

'Where ye goen?'

'Derry.'

'Why?'

'To see me Aunty Catherine.' She frowns. I don't think she believes me. She smiles an flicks her long black curly hair. I smile back. I fancy her but don't hev the courage to esk her out. Danny waits for the adults to get on. I want the bus to set aff. After a few minutes the engine starts. I cover me face an luck through me fingers as the bus gains speed near the college. Father Gallagher waalks along the path by the main door, kicken pebbles. He throws his head back, blowen out smoke. He flicks the butt onto the pebbles. His other hand rests between the chest buttons of his soutane.

Father O'Reilly stands on the tap step. His stomach seems to stick out more when he turns to look at the bus. We call him Big Art because his name is Arthur. He's so tall his thick black curly hair rubs the tap of the classroom door. He buries his wrinkled hands in the pockets of his soutane. He'll be rubben the leather strap, wonderen who he'll catch out in the Latin test. I lake Latin especially when I beat Frank at translaten sentences. Frank is good at ivrythen. I tighten me fingers together an luck away. When the bus reaches Doherty's bakery I luck back. I ken't see anybody. The bus passes Carn Hospital. It staps at the high pebble dashed wall at the front a The Convent. 'Hev a good day in Derry, won't ye,' Margaret smiles as she laves.

I smile back. I feel good. Three people are left on the bus. It chugs along the road to Glentogher. It sways wan way and then the other over the bumpy road. I grip the seat in front. No passengers or bus staps here. Only sheep. A cottage sends up trickles of black smoke. A sheepdog lies at the front. A man picks up some fresh tirf from the heather at the side of his house an stands them against each other to dry out. He presses his hands into his back as he straightens up. Me back aches lake his when Daddy takes me to do the futen in the bog. I hev to pick up all the tirf from the grass an slant them up against each other in groups a four so that the wind will dry them out. It hurts so much I hev to go down on wan knee an then swap over to the other. 'Mind what yer doen. Ye ken't stan them big bits up. They'll niver dry. Just lave them.'

A row of houses stans at the junction with Foyle Road. Lough Foyle is so near its water seems to touch the tarmac. A rusty ship with a crane belches out black smoke blocken the view a the houses on the other side a the road. Two people get on. Danny, sitten behind a glass partition, chats to them as soon as they settle into the front seat. I ken't make out what they're sayen. The bus slows down an staps outside the Customs House in Muff. Danny presses a button to open the door. Two soldiers wearen cream, green an brown uniform grip machine guns with both hands. They approach from their Land Rover. Their black boots reach above their ankles. They clomp on the steps. A badge shines on their beret above their left eye. 'Good morning,'

'Mornen,' Danny replies.

He looks at his watch. He slides his window to speak to a man in a blue uniform standen in the customs house doorway. They're just lake the wans on the news. They're big. They stare. They'll shoot me. I mustn't move. Wan soldier pointen his gun towards the floor, stans near Danny an stares. Nobody speaks. The other approaches. I want to luck away but ken't. He waalks along the passageway to the back of the bus, glancen from side to side. Nobody lucks round. The swish a his uniform rubben the seats becomes louder as he comes back. I wonder what he'll say. I don't know what to say if he esks me somethen. He'll catch on that I should be at school. He'll take me aff the bus. He'll search me. Two fat bags, big enough to hauld a loaf a bread, swing from side to side above his backside. 'Thank you,' steppen aff.

It's a quarter to ten. The bus staps an starts as it makes its way along Culmore Road an Strand Road. I smile at the Patrick Street sign on the right. Queen's Quay leads to the bus station in Foyle Street. An army hut, built a green corrugated sheets an brown sandbags, blocks the pavement on the opposite side. Metal barricades block the street. I join other people waalken along the barricades to the army hut. Ivrywan lines up wan behind the other an shuffles along. A soldier aims his rifle through a hole just big enough for his head. I jump. Another soldier haulds his rifle butt in wan hand. His other hand grips the barrel. I stare at him. I watch the people moven along. He stares at each person shufflen through the clonken bars. Nobody speaks. Some hauld out a piece of paper. Others show a small card. He checks them. The women hauld out their handbags. He must be lucken for things they've stolen. The soldier nods. Ivrywan passes through. 'Where are you going?'

'Pardon?'

'Where are you going to, I said.' He slides the barrel against my side edgen me to the wall. I think a the news on TV. I want to turn round an go home. He'll aim at me if I run.

'Just waalken round.'

'Where are you from?'

'Malin Head.'

'ID?'

'Pardon?'

'Your ID?' Me jaw tenses. Me fingers dig into me palms. I frown. I'll get back on the bus. No. If he lets me through I'll have to come back. Maybe there's another way.

'I don't understand,' shruggen my shoulders.

'Do you have any identification? Birth certificate? Passport?'

'No.' I've niver seen me birth certificate. I don't hev a passport. The soldier sighs. He pats me coat pockets. He pats me trouser pockets. He rubs me trousers down to me ankles. People shuffle behind me. They cough an grumble. He shakes his head an nods for me to kerry on. I push the turnstile bar. It clicks lake the wan at home when Daddy forces the cows into the crate. I quicken me step. I luck behind. I run.

I'm out of breath by the time I reach the next street. I luck for its name. I ken't see it. Me legs ache. I rest against a shop wall, panten. Me uncles Danny an Phelm, me cousins too. They live here. Somewhere called Pennyburn. I stare at ivry man an woman. I cover me face. I should've gone to school. The Maths an Science are nearly over now. Even if Father Campbell had leathered me it'd be over in seconds.

I waalk to the corner. A jeep, painted green an brown with wire mesh on the windscreen, blocks the pavement. Two soldiers stand in front a the bonnet. I cross to the other side. I turn left onto Shipquay Street. People dash in an out of a large shop. I go in an waalk between the rows. People rush up an down between shelves a soaps, bulbs, magazines, cards, records, towels an clothes. They stand on their toes to reach the top. They put things in the basket. I turn right. I turn left. People queue near a counter. A lady taps nonstap on the till. It's faster than Mary Anne's. It makes less noise. It has more keys.

I waalk out into the street. I luck for its name. "Cable Street". I stand an luck round wonderen which way to go. People rush past me. I stare. No sign of me uncles or cousins. Cars stap an start. Engines rev. I cover me nose. A cinema with flashen lights across the entrance catches me eye. *The Sound of Music* showing 12pm. I luck at me watch. Half past eleven. I push the glass door. It turns round. It keeps on turnen.

'How ye doen there?'

'The Sound of Music, please.'

'One Shilling and sixpence.' I hand her the two shillings Jack Merchant gave me two weeks ago for helpen him with the hay. She lucks at the money an tuts. She pushes the change to me. I buy a packet a rollos an head to the door. A man shines a torch along the aisle. I settle into a soft red armchair. People whisper. Wrappers rattle. The screen flashes. Loud music starts. The screen is so big I hev to move me eyes up, down an side to side to see all a it. It's bigger than the wan in Culdaff where I go at the weekend. A lady dances an smiles on the tap of a hill covered in grass an heather. A village lies below. The sun shines. She starts singen. 'The hills are alive with the sound of music…'

I don't lake this. It's boren. Nothen's happenen. I can't stay here. I need to get out. No. I better stay here. Nobody'll see me. I wait. I watch. I look round. I check me watch every few minutes. I'll go at a quarter to two to get back to the bus station in time. Time passes so slowly. I step out onto the street. I head back to the army checkpoint. The same soldier is at the turnstile. He nods an lets me through. I get on the bus. 'Had a good day then, Patrick?' esks Danny.

'Yes,' walken to the back seat a the bus. He lucks at me in the mirror. I luck out the window. He knows.

'I should charge ye for this trip ye know. Yer ticket is only for school,' Jim says punchen my ticket.

I smile. I say nothen. He stands by the windscreen near the little metal door that Danny shuts when he sits at the steeren wheel. They chat. I ken't make out what they're sayen. Jim lucks back at me from time to time. They're taalken about me. They'll tell The College. They'll tell Mammy an Daddy. Father O'Reilly'll cane me. Mammy'll send me to boarden school lake Kevin.

At twenty past two Danny shuts the door a the bus an edges onto Foyle Street. A man an a woman sit in the front seat. I'll hev to write a note for Big Art tomorrow. I'll hev to luck in her writen pad. I'll hev to tear out a piece a paper. 'Dear Reverend Father O'Reilly, Patrick wasn't at school yesterday because he had a high temperature.' No. 'Dear Reverend Father O'Reilly, Patrick was absent from school yesterday because he had a bad toothache.' I'll practise when I get back to me bedroom. I'll hev to steal an envelope from the tap drawer in the dresser. She'll be in the kitchen an scullery all evenen. I'll hev to use me own paper. Father O'Reilly might suspect somethen.

The bus slows down an staps at The Convent. Margaret an Roisin get on. They smile. They sit beside each other an chat. I fancy Roisin too. She smiles at me most days. I don't know what to say. I think she lakes me too. I think of the school ceilidh at Ballyliffin. She esked me to dance with her for the *Siege of Ennis*. She kept squeezen me hand. I shud've said somethen. I cud've esked her if she wanted a coke or lemonade but the priests were watchen.

'Ye just comen home now?' Margaret esks.

'How's yer auntie?'

I stare at her. What's she taalken about? 'Oh. Oh. She's doen ok now.' Margaret stares. She whispers to Roisin. Roisin lucks back at me. They whisper agen. The bus staps in Carn at three o'clock. The man an woman get aff. Danny sits an reads a book. I think I'll get aff. I can waalk round a bit. I'll mix in better with ivrywan from The College an Tech. They arrive in groups. They chat. They laugh. They push an shove along the footpath. The McCarthy boys run to the door. They squash to get on.

'Get back, ye clowns,' Danny shouts. 'Or ye'll hev te waalk home.'

They waalk to the backseat sniggeren. I stare out the window. Dick Mariner has moved the red cloth of the ice cream machine. I want to buy a ninety-nine. I don't hev enough money. I've got six rollos left. I'll eat them in me room. I'll stay there pretenden I'm doen me homework. I'll play with me pens an biros in the blue missions box I used to put pennies in for the African babies afore I cut the lid aff. Mammy'll hev got the fire ready.

'You need a few sticks. One firelighter and brown turf first. It's light and catches quick. Coal's too heavy and hard. Just let it burn a wee while. Then throw on a couple of bits of black turf and coal,' she'd say kneelen on wan knee.

I think about pushen me table aside an pullen the chair up to the grate. The yellow, blue an red flames licken their way in, out through the tirf an up the chimley. The petrol smell a the fire lighter. The bits a wood turnen brown an black lake burnt toast. Hissen. Spitten. Me feet danglen. Me hands hoveren over the flames.

At ten past four Danny staps at The Square Toe. I sneak round the back a Iona House. I ken't see anywan. I grab me coat an bag. I waalk past Michael Paddy Brian's house. A bicycle lies against the wall a Mary Anne's shop. I'm not goen in for the sweets she gives me on the way home. She'll still be cross with me after what happened last week.

'Well, Patrick, what hev ye bin larnen the day?'

'Just stuff.'

'Here y'are now. A wee sweet or two. Don't eat 'em afore yer dinner or yer Mammy'll not be too happy.'

'I won't.'

'How's yer Mammy and Daddy anyway?'

'Daddy died yesterday.'

'Oh, Jesus, Mary an Joseph, Patrick,' screamen an cuppen her hand over the mouth. She pushed up her glasses with a scrunched tissue to catch the tear resten on the rim. She let them slide back agen.

'What happened?'

'Not sure. Just died.'

'May God have mercy on his soul.'

'I'm only joken. He's not dead at all.'

'Oh Jesus. Mary an Joseph, Patrick.' I grabbed the sweets. She lunges across the counter, flailen her arms, to hit me. I duck an run. I waalk along the road lucken into the fiels on both sides. I ken't see Daddy. I peep between the whin bushes. I luck towards the barn. He's not there. I tiptoe in the front door an head down the hall. I drop me bag by the table leg in me room. The flames in the grate lick the back of the fireplace. The room feels warm. I head to the kitchen.

'Had a good day at school then?' I stare. Mammy's niver esked me afore.

'Hmmmmm. Ok.'

'What did you do?'

'I had a test in Latin. Got good marks. I hated the Maths,' staren at the plate.

'Have you seen Daddy yet?' I freeze.

'No.'

I luck at her. Me eyes bulge. Me teeth clench. She bangs the plate of sausages, cabbage, carigeen moss an potatoes in front of me without speaken. I take a mouthful. The fork trembles. I don't want to chew. 'Why weren't you at school?'

I stare at the plate. I don't speak. She bends over me. I try to work out how she knows. If I don't speak I'm in trouble. If I tell the truth I'm in trouble. If I tell lies I'll be in more trouble. 'I rang The College to get you to go to the vets to collect a cow's dose Daddy ordered. Veronica told me you weren't there. Where were you?'

I stare at my plate.

'Where were you?'

'Derry.'

'Derry? What in God's name? There's been riots. You stupid boy,' raisen her hand to hit me. I duck.

Daddy appears at the back door. He stares at me. I take another mouthful. He dips a cup in the bucket of fresh water from the well, swallows an puts it on the table. Mammy thumps the water with the scouren pad as she scrubs the potato pot. He shuts the door an laves.

'For God's sake, Patrick, the British soldiers are on the streets now. It was on the news. Where d'you get the money from anyway?'

'Jack Merchant.'

'Don't believe you. He's a Protestant.' I luck sideways. She glares at me. 'Count your lucky stars Daddy believed me. I told him I couldn't get through on Mary Anne's phone. He got James to go,' peepen through the window to make sure Daddy wouldn't hear. Me eyes bulge. I tighten me grip on the knife an fork.

'You didn't tell him?' She shakes her head. Her eyes redden.

'Patrick, you do that again, I'll not only tell him but you'll be going to the Brothers like Kevin.

Inishowen

A few miles outside Derry the road signs and speed limits changed to be written in Irish, English and kilometres. *Céad Míle Fáilte* welcomed me to Donegal. When I was a boy my neighbour Robbie said that the garda didn't bother much about speeding. According to my family it was a different story now. I kept to the speed limit. I turned on the radio. I tuned into a man reading the eleven o'clock news on Radio Eireann in a Dublin accent. I followed the signs for Muff. The new wide road wound its way along the banks of Lough Foyle. A rusty boat carrying metal crates crawled towards the city. I thought about the day I sat on the Lough Swilly Bus playing truant in Derry. Danny driving. Jim grumping up and down the aisle as he punched tickets. Margaret asking me where I was going. I don't think she ever found out I was skipping school.

    The mist, hiding the top of Slieve Snacht, began to evaporate as I drove through Glentogher on my way to Carndonagh. The sheep no longer strolled in clusters along the roadside, nibbling the wind-beaten blades of scutch grass. A newly white-plastered, detached house imposed its incongruent design into the landscape. A shining black jeep stood by its UPVC frosted glass front door. The playing fields where I used to play Gaelic football were now a housing estate. The prefabricated chalet where Mr. O'Leary strapped me for cheating in History had been demolished and the toilet block, where I sometimes hid from Mr. Campbell's Maths and Science lessons, was flattened.

    I drove up the steep slope of Pound Street past the demolished shirt factory and alongside the new Tesco supermarket to the junction with Malin Street. Doherty's Café was still selling ninety nines made from local milk. Mariner's sweet and ice cream shop, where I used to meet my girlfriend, Rita, at lunchtimes, was no longer there. At the end of the street the red roof tiles of the Lilac Ballroom had faded. I used to pick her up from her home on Saturday evenings in my father's Ford Poplar car. I'd sneak out of the house with his car keys and return them at one in the morning. The steering wheel was so loose the car wobbled from side to side. He must have known I took it. I wondered why he never said anything.

Interview

On Saturday I watch him coming out of Mary Anne's shop, freewheeling down the brae past the piggery on his black bicycle with raised handlebars lake the horns of the bull in The Moss Field. When he turns into our lane I grip my hands with excitement. He leans his bicycle against the evergreen hedge. He lifts his postbag over his head knocking his peaked cap to wan side. His arm delves in up to his elbow an digs out two letters.

'Good mornen, Lizzie. Just a couple for ye th'day,' handing her a large brown envelope an a small white one. The postman tips his cap at Mammy, checks his bicycle clips an swings his leg over the seat. His arms shake as he balances on the cracked leather seat held together with black tape. 'Bye now,' without looking round an waving his arm while the other steadies the handlebars.

Yes! A brown envelope. 'No. Nothing for you, Patrick,' she says running a knife along the flap. 'Another missions magazine asking for money,' sliding it onto the folded Derry Journal on her brown leatherette stool.

Every day on the way home on the bus I imagine Mammy'll have left a letter on my table. I go straight to my room. Nothing there. They don't want me. I'm not good enough. I need to apply somewhere else. I don't want to go anywhere else. I want John an Kevin from my class to come to De La Salle in Manchester with me. I hope they apply. Even though John is from Buncrana I lake him because we play Gaelic Football for the school team. I lake Kevin because his Daddy sometimes drives the school bus.

'Patrick, there's a letter for you.' It's a brown rectangular shape with my name an address written in black ink. I open it. My hands shake. I look at Mammy. She smiles. I open the folded white sheets of paper.

'What's it say?'

'Dear Patrick, thank you for your application to study at De La Salle College of Education. I would like to invite you for interview on Thursday 18th May at 1.30pm. The interview will be…

'I've got an interview.'

'Let me see it.' She reads. She hands it back to me. She smiles. 'Well, congratulations. I knew you'd do it.'

Daddy comes in for his tea. I grab the letter an run to my room. When I go to school the next day, I run to John an Kevin. 'I've got an interview.'

'Yea, I got one too,' John replies. 'We might end up playing football together.'

'I don't think there'll be a Gaelic team there.'

'I've got an interview as well but I'm not going,' Kevin says. 'I'm thinking of applying to Limerick University.'

'My Daddy wants me to stay at home and help with his fruit and vegetable shop but I'm not doing that,' John says.

John and myself stand by the main school gate waiting for Father O'Reilly to arrive in his Ford Zephyr. He is the principal of the college. He teaches me Honours Leaving Certificate Latin. Its silver grille with double headlights appears at the corner of Bridge Street. It eases to the edge of the pavement, scattering the lose clippings. 'Right boys. Get in,' winding down the window.

His thick black hair brushes the roof. Half his forehead hides above the door frame. He wafts the cigarette smoke away. With the door half-open he crushes the cigarette butt on the tarmac. I sink into the soft red leather seat. 'Ready?' looking in his rear-view mirror. We nod. We don't speak. I stare straight ahead. I push my hands under my legs. The leather stitching scrapes my knuckles. Father O'Reilly slides the column change lever upwards. The Ford Zephyr eases forwards with a slight hum. His fat brown spotty hand moves the lever up and down until the car's in top gear. His sleeves slide up his arm. His square-faced, silver bracelet wristwatch glistens. I think of how he removed it before he strapped me for Latin mistakes.

The car sways over the bumps so smoothly it feels lake we're floating on air. We clear our throats. A low conversation comes from the radio. I wiggle my backside. The leather farts. We snigger. I think of the red Ford Zephyr James used to have with its twin headlamps, wide silver grille, white wheels an a black leather bench seat in the front. I remember the day he had to rush to the vets in Carndonagh for a dying cow's medicine. I remember the roar of the double bore exhaust on his way back as he tore round the corner at Michael Paddy Brian's, Big Denis' an Mary Anne's Shop. He shot down the brae past the piggery so fast I thought he wouldn't be able to turn the corner. The car screeched up to the front of our house an tilted, scattering gravel into the hedge. Laddie ran with his tail between his legs. James smiled as he opened the door. He smiled at me, pleased with his driven.

Father O'Reilly slows down as he approaches the Customs at Muff. An armed soldier an a customs officer came towards us. 'Mornen, Father,' says the customs officer peering into the car. He smiles at us. We smile back.

'Ok, Father. That's fine,' tilting his hat.

The radio crackles along Culmore Road. The green, white, gold, green, white, gold on the kerb stones on both sides of the road near Derry flash past us as Father O'Reilly drives along. I don't remember seeing them before. People must've got paint on their shoes when it was fresh. What a lot of paint it must've taken. Further along, a red, white an blue flag flaps. Kerb stones painted red, white an blue decorate the footpath. Army jeeps crawl along. Soldiers stand at corners ready to shoot.

Once out of Derry, the Ford Zephyr speeds towards Belfast. It's half past twelve. I should be waiting for Rita at Mariner's Shop. I won't see her for months if I go to Manchester. She might meet somebody else at the dances in the Culdaff Arms on Saturdays. I can't leave her.

Father O'Reilly lifts the metal knocker an bangs it twice. Footsteps clatter. The chain clinks. The lock clonks. The latch clicks. The door opens. A lady pokes her head round the edge staring over her gold rimmed glasses. 'Can I help you?' looking up at Father O'Reilly.

'I've brought two pupils for interviews with Brother Austin.'

'Oh. Come on in, Father.' She steps back, bows an opens the door wide. 'This way,' pointing with her arm. She bows again. Her black leather shoes clatter towards a dark brown door on the left. She bows once again an extends her hand, inviting us to enter. 'I'll tell Brother Austin you're here, Father,' closing the door behind her.

'You can sit down, boys. Don't suppose Brother Austin will mind. Remember what I told you to say.' We nod as we sink into the black leather couch. I twirl the leather buttons on the armrest. The grandfather clock in the corner breaks the silence. Father O'Reilly sits opposite on the other side of the dark brown coffee table with a glass top. The brown an green rug slips under his feet. He bends his head back to look at the brown bookshelves filled to the ceiling. The door opens. 'Stand up, boys,' pushing himself off the armchair.

'Good to see you, Arthur.' Their soutanes swish as they meet in the middle of the room and shake hands.

'And you too, Brother Austin.' He stares at us.

'You are?' extending his hand.

'I'm John, Brother Austin,' He nods an steps sideways towards me.

'And you are?' his blue eyes staring at me.

'I'm Patrick, Brother Austin,' staring up at him.

I look at Father O'Reilly an back at Brother Austin. Grey hairs grow from his nostrils. He grips my hand an nods. His skin is cold an clammy. Blue veins run between his knuckles. I shiver. I wonder if he has a strap in his pocket. He shuffles sideways. Brother Austin approaches Father O'Reilly. 'I suppose alphabetical order is the easiest way.' Father O'Reilly nods. 'I'll start with John,' indicating with a nod of the head for him to follow.

I sit down. Father O'Reilly walks back and forth along the wall of books. The grandfather clock in the corner bongs half past one. It's twenty to two. Come on, John, get out. Don't keep us waiting. I rub my hands together. They sweat. Father O'Reilly strolls to the bay window with his hands linked behind his back just as he does when he tests us. It's a quarter to two. The door opens. John enters staring at the floor. His skin is pale. He sits down beside me. He shakes his head.

'Right, Patrick, follow me,' says the lady edging out the door with a smile. I quicken my step. Her blue skirt sways from side to side near her ankles. She taps the door twice edging her ear towards a golden plate with *Brother Austin* inscribed in black capitals.

'Come in.' She turns the knob, pushes the door an indicates with her hand for me to enter. The door shuts behind me. 'Welcome, Patrick,' holding out his hand. He stands behind a shining, wooden, brown table with curved legs. A black telephone sits on the corner. He looks bigger now with the bay window behind him. Papers lie on a leather square on his desk. It looks like my application. A clock ticks. I force a smile. I rehearse the advice Father O'Reilly gave me. Sit up straight. Don't cross your legs. Smile.

'Please take a seat,' pointing to the brown chair with the tall back and soft seat. I sit down without moving it. I place my feet together an rest my hands on my lap. The tight tie an new tweed jacket Mammy bought me make me feel warm an uncomfortable. 'Tell me a little about yourself, Patrick.'

I didn't prepare for this. I don't know what to say. John should've warned me. I think about my school, my family an what I want to study at college. 'I go to The College in Carndonagh and am waiting on my Honours Leaving Certificate results. I live in Malin Head an have seven brothers, Brother.'

'What subjects are you studying?'

'French, Latin an Geography, Brother.'

'Interesting. What do you like to read?' I remember what Father O'Reilly told me about reading a book for the interview. If I tell him I never read I'll be telling the truth but that won't impress him. 'I've just read *Hard Times*.'

'What did you think of it?' I can't tell him I didn't lake it. It's the first novel I've read. I don't lake reading because I'm not quick enough in class. I don't want to read any more books.

'I laked it,' hoping he wouldn't ask anything else.

'So you want to do French and P.E.?' I give a quiet sigh of relief that the book question is out of the way.

'Yes, Brother.'

'What sports do you like?'

'Gaelic Football. I play for the school team, Brother.' The veins on the back of his scrawny right hand seem thicker than they were earlier. He flicks through my application with one hand an rests his chin in the palm of the other. No more questions. Please. Let me go. Brother Austin takes a deep breath.

'Any other sports?'

'I like running. I enjoy the school cross country.'

'What about gymnastics?'

'No. I've not done gymnastics.'

'We have a strong gymnastics team in each year an we compete against other colleges. Would you be keen to take part?'

'Yes. Brother Austin.' I hope he doesn't ask me about swimming. I can't swim. He won't let me do P.E. I should've learned in the river on the farm. I could've gone to the shore in the summer lake Mammy told me to. I didn't want the neighbours to see me.

'Well, I will be in touch soon. Probably within a week,' closing my application form. He stands up an shakes my hand. His skin is warmer now. He forces a smile. When I open the door the lady is standing opposite. She smiles an scuttles down the hallway ahead of me to the waiting room.

On Tuesday Mammy's standing at the door when I come home from school. 'This is for you.' Patrick Doherty, Crega, Malin Head, Ballygorman P.O, Lifford, County Donegal, Ireland in black capital letters on a large brown envelope. I grab a knife from the kitchen. I pull out the folded white sheets of paper. 'What's it say?'

I read.

'Tell me. What's it say?'

'I got in.'

'Congratulations. You deserve it.' Turning away she heads into her bedroom an closes the door. I sit in the kitchen. I want her to come out.

Malin Head

A new roundabout, constructed on the sites of the former potato factory and abandoned bus station, surprised me. I circled the roundabout twice looking for the way to Malin Town. How ridiculous, I thought, having been through this town by car and bus all my life, I should know where to go. The road curved at McSheffrey's Bridge over Trawbreaga Bay. A boy in my class drove his car into the water there killing the woman with him.

Within a quarter of a mile the road changed from a white-lined, wide and smooth surface to a three mile stretch of sunken tracks on both sides of a tarred road. Apart from a few repaired patches, the bumps and potholes seemed the same as they had always been. The road, raised about three feet above the fields, narrowed as I approached Malin Town. Deep tyre tracks on the grass verge and a crater of fresh soil showed me where my father's car had plunged over the edge. What Theresa had said me now made sense.

A few yards further along sunken scars in the field revealed how the car had nosedived. Deep furrows between wide tractor tracks showed where the car had been dragged. Stretches of broken tar and loose chippings, crushed and whitened by a heavy lifting machine, marked the road. I couldn't understand how Mammy had survived in the front passenger seat. What she must've gone through when the car swerved and my father hadn't answered her shouts. She said it all happened so quickly. He knew nothing about it. I wanted to stop but couldn't. My father was dead. Mammy and Aunt Mary Logue could've died too. I wanted to see the damage to him.

I followed the coastal road along Trawbreaga Bay where local men used to fish for crabs and mussels to supplement their farming income. The Isle of Doagh across the bay, idyllic with its Atlantic beaches, holiday homes and patchwork fields. A mile further along, St. Mary's Church, the second most northerly church in Ireland stood among the highest sand dunes in western Europe. It was close by to Five Fingers Strand where the IRA had buried Kalashnikovs and fifty thousand rounds of ammunition. My father would be laid to rest in the cemetery here along with all my other relatives.

I drove on to Malin Head, the island of Ireland's famed most northerly point. I pulled into The Star of the Sea church carpark. I looked at the tall roof and wondered how my brother John had got up there to repair it. I thought of the story he had told about how two local men coming home from the pub moved the foundation markers to make the new church bigger. According to him the church was built without anyone knowing the markers had been moved. I wound down the window to get a clearer view of my home. The front door was open. A black car and a blue jeep were parked along the trimmed hedge.

I drove on past The Square Toe. A green telephone box stood where I used to wait for the Lough Swilly bus to take me to The College. I drove past Dock's Lane and John Joe's shop. I thought about the cigarettes that Liam and Danny, from the National School, had made me steal on the way home from school and the whin bushes we hid behind when they shouted 'Guinness is good for you' at Miss McGuinness.

My brother told me Liam had taken to the drink and had died young of a heart attack. Danny married and earns money from seasonal fishing. I continued towards the National School. The garden we used to weed was covered in tar to make the playground bigger. I turned left onto The New Road. The Atlantic waves spewed over the rocks. Spume shot up and scattered. The whin bushes and rushes bent in the sea breeze. The new White Strand B and B stood where Michael Bulbin's thatched cottage used to be. Across the field the tarred roof of my brother James' new shed towered over the old byres.

I looped around by the shore and turned right into our lane. I parked near the old ploughs and reapers that James had so painstakingly restored. The evergreen hedge by the whitewashed wall at the front of the house wasn't green anymore. Short stumpy branches stuck out. The two 'L' shaped iron hinges protruded from the pillars where the blue wooden gate used to squeak. Two oval shaped water marks on the step by the front door showed where two white, sand-filled, plastic ducks used to face each other. The plastic handle of the new UPVC white door was cold. I remembered the brass knob and the old cream wooden door. I used to sneak through it unnoticed when I got home from school. I pushed through the new door.

The old statue of Our Lady, with the holy water font at her feet, still hung on the door frame. I dipped my finger in it and made the sign of the cross. How many fingers had dipped into it and how many visitors had Mammy sprinkled with it? She had sprinkled holy water on me as I left for Manchester when I was a student and on Sheila, the girls and I, as we left after summer holidays.

The oak coat and umbrella stand with Mammy's coats and headscarves faced me. I glanced in the mirror. I looked at the brown and yellow quarry floor tiles. I used to tiptoe out to dances on Friday nights. I inhaled mothballed air. Behind the door the old public black telephone box, once attached to the wall in Aunty Mary Anne's shop, was screwed onto the cream plaster where James had fixed it.

Mary Anne and Barney used to lay a long pole with a black coat fixed to the top and lean it against their whitewashed gable as a sign to tell Mammy that someone had left a phone message for her. One of us would eventually notice the coat and rush to the shop for the message.

When she wanted to ring my brother Willie, in Chicago, she'd go to the shop, ring *Mrs. Post Office* and book a call for the following day. Mammy would return the next day with a purse full of coins. 'Put your money in now,' Mrs. Post Office would say. The coins would thump to the bottom of the metal box. The phone would burr. 'Putting you through now.' After a few minutes, she'd interrupt Mammy and tell her that she had a minute left.

I picked up the receiver from the small table at the side of the metal box. The phone worked.

Cahir

I sit at me table in me bedroom at five o'clock. I'm studyen for me Honours Leaving Cert. The rain batters on the window. The wind hisses. The top pane rattles. I pick up pieces of coal with the gold-coloured tongs an drop them onto the dyen flames. Sparks shoot up. Cinders crumble an faal through the grate. I stretch out me hands. I rub them together. I finish the volcano diagram for Geography an translate the ten sentences into Latin. I pick up the blue missions' box from the shelf underneath my table. I empty out the pieces of the two fountain pens. The nibs are dry. I hold the suction rubber an dip the tip into the bottle of blue ink. I press the rubber an release it. I press again. Ink seeps in. I screw the pen together. I try to write. The bent nip scrapes the piece of paper. I press the tip hard to line up its two points. One snaps. A blob of ink spreads. The tip tears the paper. I screw it up an throw it in the bin.

The gravel at the front of the house rattles. It must be James driven the tractor. I want to go out. I want to drive. I hate hiden in here. Mammy an Daddy think I'm worken hard for me cert. All I do is come home, have me dinner, come in here, do me homework an kill time till bedtime. I walk along the hallway to James' room at the end an look out the window. A red car stands by the front gate. Cahir walks up the cement path to the front door followed by a priest. He's supposed to be in Maynooth trainen to be a priest. Mammy never said he was comen home. I tiptoe back along the hallway. I stop at the hall door an listen.

'Hello, Cahir. This is a surprise,' says Mammy openen the front door.

'Hello, Mrs. Doherty. I'm Father McGuire. I'm Cahir's supervisor.'

'Hello, Father. Is there something wrong?'

'Well, I think we need to talk.'

'Come in. Please come in.'

The front door shuts. The kitchen door shuts. I wait. Silence. I squeeze the hall door handle so that it won't squeak. I tiptoe forward to the kitchen door. I can't make out what Father McGuire's sayen. I put my ear to the door. 'Cahir's decided he's leaving the priesthood. We've had many discussions over the past few weeks. He's sure it's the right thing for him.'

'Oh, Jesus, Mary and Joseph. All these years I've waited for you to be ordained. Five years your Daddy and myself have scrimped and saved and now you do this. What's Daddy going to say?'

'I'm sorry, Mammy. I'm really sorry. I didn't know how to tell you. I didn't want to disappoint you.' I never heard him cry before. He takes deep breaths. He groans. Somebody bangs the table.

'Disappoint me? What'll the neighbours say? And Mrs. Post Office. Her son, Philip was ordained last year.'

A chair scrapes the floor. Somethen bangs against the top in the scullery. Water flows. It thumps on the cooker. Cups rattle. A drawer rasps. A cupboard door slams. Mammy whimpers. 'I prayed for the day you'd say your first Mass in the chapel. I always longed to be the first person to receive Holy Communion from you. All of Malin Head would've come. There would've been a big party in the hall like Father Philip. I'd have died happy. What'll I tell Father Kelly?'

The kettle hisses. Water pours. She shuffles. She groans. The cups an saucers rattle on the tray. 'What do we do now, Father?'

'The best thing, I think, is for Cahir to come back with me for a few days so that everyone has time to think. There's no need to rush into anything.'

'What d'you mean? No rush. I can't go on like this for God's sake.' A cup bangs on a saucer. Mammy's shoes clatter. I dash down the hallway. The back door opens. Mammy rushes past my window. I wait. I listen.

'Willie,' she shouts at the top of her voice.

I stare at the window. I wait. Mammy rushes back past my window. She slams the back door. Daddy shuffles past my window, his head bowed. He slams the back door. I put my ear to my bedroom door. I want to go back to the hall door. I better not. Mammy's angry. Daddy'll be angry too. I'm safer here. The kitchen an front doors open. Mammy an Father McGuire speak but I can't make out what they're sayen. I tiptoe back into James' room.

Cahir an Father McGuire get into the car. Cahir looks round. He wipes his eyes. The car sets aff. The front door shuts. I go back into my room. It's a quarter past seven. I sit an stare. I think back to when Cahir left The Colgan Hall College with his Honours Leaving Certificate an I was starten in September.

Mammy was so delighted when he was accepted into Maynooth Seminary. I remember her taken him duren the summer to visit McDonagh Stores in Carndonagh to buy black shoes an black socks, then to the shops in Buncrana for a black overcoat, black scarf, two black shirts an a black suit. Finally, she went to the Derry shops to buy two black soutanes, rosary beads an a leather backed bible. 'Cahir, try this on again,' she'd say taken wan soutane out of the wrapper when she arrived home. 'I want to make sure it fits properly in case I have to take it back.'

He left his book on the chair in the kitchen an shuffled into the sitten room. He stood in the doorway. He looked an stared. 'Come here and try this soutane on,' she'd say as she flicked her wrist to make him hurry up. She opened it wide an held it up to her face. He pulled a his jumper, turned round an slid his arms into the sleeves. She stretched it over his shoulders. 'Turn around. Let's have a look at you. Oh, that fits you well. You look good in it,' pullen the sides an buttonen the soutane from his neck down to his shoes. 'How's it feel?'

Cahir shrugged his shoulders. I looked at the black soutane coveren his shoelaces. He looked taller an thinner. He looked at me. I thought of Father Kelly swaggeren into primary school with his soutane swayen round his feet an shouten at us. Cahir might do that. He'd shout from the altar. I wouldn't lake my brother to be a priest. I wouldn't know whether to call him Cahir or Father. If he came to Malin Head I'd have to go to him for Confession an Holy Communion.

I remember walken past the sitten room every day and peepen in. All the items lay wrapped in clear plastic bags on the settee an two armchairs. Camphor filled the air. 'Oh, come and have a look at what I've got Cahir for Maynooth,' Mammy'd say to anywan who came to the house. She'd scuttle in, open the bags an hold up the items. She'd turn them over an show off the label an the linen.

As the day approached for him to go, more an more items appeared. Blue pyjamas, brown towels, black shoe polish, black sandals, black gloves an a black umbrella. A brown suitcase lay open on the floor. He wandered round the house. He didn't smile. He didn't speak. I thought of when Father Kelly used to come into my primary school an talked to the boys about goen to the priesthood. He talked to the girls about goen to the Convent secondary school in Carndonagh an then goen to be nuns. He gave us glossy leaflets with pictures of priests worken with children in Africa. 'Fill in the form on the back and post it off', he'd say. 'You'll get more information in a few days.'

On the mornen Cahir was due to leave Mammy got him up early. She made him have a bath. She laid a fresh change of clothes on his bed. Joe Gorman, the taxi man, arrived at nine o'clock. He put Cahir's suitcase in the boot. Mammy stood on the front doorstep. Cahir put his arm round her. He stared at me. As he closed the car door Daddy came out of the barn. He stood near Mammy. He stared. He swallowed. He didn't speak. Cahir looked straight ahead. Mammy grabbed the holy water font from the sitten room door frame. She dipped her finger in an sprinkled it on the car. The car set off. Mammy an Daddy waved. The car drove past Mary Anne's shop. It turned the corner at Michael Paddy Brian's house. It disappeared. Mammy bowed her head an went back inside. She shut the door. Daddy turned away an shuffled on the gravel back to the barn. I stood an waited for the car to turn right at The Square Toe. Its blue roof shone through the bushes. I looked towards the carpark outside the chapel. I waited. The car revved as it climbed the hill. It disappeared. I made the sign of the cross an headed back to me room.

Mooney's Bar

I stand at the double door of Mooney's Bar. *Mooney's* is written in an arc at the top of the glass of the left-hand side door and *Bar* on the right. I press against the handle and go up four wooden steps. A mixture of beer and furniture polish smells fill the air; the lights behind the bar reflecting in the mirrors contrast with the unlit lounge. The legs of four stools reach my chest as they stand against the tubular footrest running the full length of the bar. My fingers feel the cracks in their thick, circular, leather seats. A black rubber mat, like a miniature doormat with holes, lies near the end of the bar. A black towel with *London Pride* printed in yellow hangs over a pump handle. On the top glass shelf stand bottles of different shapes and colours. Below them there's a row of bottles upside down. A gadget with a short, thin, silver pipe is pushed into the neck. I don't know why the liquid doesn't run out. The reflection on the mirrored wall dazzles my eyes.

On the worktop rest more bottles with a thin silver spout, a plate of lemons, a glass of wooden, finger-length and needle-thin sticks and a breadboard. Below the worktop bottles fill the shelves. Behind a glass fridge door stand cans of beer. Bottles lie on wire racks. I'll never learn all this. I should be honest and tell the manager I never worked in Marner's Café in Carndonagh. He's bound to check. He'll find out anyway when he sees how hopeless I'll be. I just hope that what the agency said about him wanting an Irish person is right. Footsteps clatter down the stairs at the back of the bar. 'Hello. Can I help?' says the man in a white, short-sleeved shirt, waddling toward me. 'I'm Terry, the manager. You must be Patrick.'

'Yes, I am.'

'Well, this is the bar area as you can see. There's the lounge,' pointing to the end of the bar. 'There's another bar and lounge downstairs but we only open that in the evenings. The kitchen's upstairs where all the meals are cooked. Follow me. You can choose whatever you want from the fridge for your lunch once you start,' opening the fridge door.

'Thank you,' I say bending my head back to see the top shelf. He must be offering me the job. He's not asked me anything yet. I thought I'd have another interview like the one with Brother Austin. 'Let's find Hughie. He's the cellar man. Just hold your nose when he talks to you.'

Hughie appears at the top of the cellar stairs. Braces hold up his brown, baggy, corduroy trousers. A cigarette droops from the corner of his mouth. 'Hughie meet Patrick. He's come to see about the job.' He extends his hand. I shake it and pull away. Sweat seeps through his red and green checked shirt under his arm. He says something but I don't understand. I nod and smile. 'Hughie'll show you the cellar.'

He scuttles down the stairs flicking the ash from his cigarette. 'This is it. My cell, I call it. I spend most of my time here. These damaged cans. We can't sell them. That's my little stash.' I nod. I smile. He's speaking too fast. I don't want to speak. He won't understand me. 'Here, take this,' handing me a crate of beer bottles. 'Follow me.'

Hughie drops his crate at the top of the stairs, bends over and splutters. He rubs his sleeve across his forehead. I turn away. 'The boss won't let me stay up here,' straightening himself up.

'Well, you've seen everything now, Patrick,' Terry calls from the end of the bar.

'Yes, thank you.'

'I tell you what. You can start on a trial basis tomorrow for a week and we'll take it from there. How's that sound?'

'That's brilliant.' I smile and shake his hand.

I toss and turn in bed. The orange streetlights shine through the curtains. I hope I don't see Hughie tomorrow. I think I'll vomit if he comes near me again. I'm not surprised Jim makes him stay in the cellar. I should be safe enough in the bar. I'll need to stay near Jim to learn everything.

I arrive at Mooney's Bar at nine o'clock. The smell of beer and polish seems less. Footsteps clatter down the stairs from the kitchen. I hope it isn't Hughie. Terry appears. 'Hello, so you've decided to come back.' His accent sounds like Dublin where my brother-in-law comes from.

'Yes.'

'You looked terrified yesterday. I thought I wouldn't see you again.'

'I'm scared. Never been in a pub before. I'm a Pioneer.'

'What? An Irish man who doesn't touch the hard stuff? Sure you'll be drinkin in no time.'

I hope he's wrong. I don't want to drink. I don't like the smell of it. I'm scared what Daddy'll do if he finds out. 'I don't think so. Nobody in my family drinks.'

'Stay with me and you'll be fine. Us Irish men'll stick together,' leading me behind the bar. 'These are the pumps for the beer,' resting his hand on top of a handle.

'You just put the glass under the nozzle and pull the handle slowly. We'll have a practice in a few minutes. Over here you'll see the pint glasses for beers, and these are half pints. One or two chaps like these heavy mugs but they'll tell you. This tankard's Jim's. He's first here every day. You can't miss him. He sits on that stool with his pipe, tin of tobacco and newspaper til closing time. In all the years I've been here I've never seen him going to the loo. I don't know how he manages. These ones hanging down are for wine and brandy. Oh, these trays, they're slop trays to catch any beer that spills from the glasses. If it's a stranger, we tip some into a glass and then top it up from the pump. For God's sake, don't do it unless I'm here. These are the optics. Teachers Whisky is popular,' pointing to the upside-down bottles.

I've heard of opticians but not optics. I don't know what he means. I want to ask but don't. 'The Americans like it. They think it's the proper stuff. They don't cotton on to the cheap stuff I put in. Now, you keep that to yourself,' pointing his finger. 'Well, there you have it, more or less, Patrick. Any questions?' I shake my head. I remember nothing apart from the slop trays. I want to ask him to repeat everything.

'Terry!' a woman's voice shouts from the kitchen.

He rushes upstairs. It's ten forty. Jim'll be at the door in twenty minutes. I hope Terry's back before he comes. I step backwards and forwards, turn right and left, look up and down and glance side to side. Fosters XXXX. Martini. Jack Daniels. Calvados. Crème de Menthe. Courvoisier. London Pride. Kronenbourg. I wonder what Jim drinks. Perhaps it's a bottle of beer or Guinness. Daddy used to call it stout but I never knew the difference. I remember smelling it as a child and never forgot the stink. I look at the bottles through the fridge door. I put a pint glass under the nozzle. I'm not sure whether it should stay near the top of the glass or sink to the bottom. I push the glass up. The pump's black handle stretches up to my forehead. I pull it gently. It's stiff. I apply more pressure until it's horizontal. A cream froth starts to bubble from the nozzle. It gurgles. The froth rises. The bubbles grow bigger. A brown liquid settles at the bottom. I ease the pressure of the handle. It returns to its upright position.

A man rattles the door and cups his hands round his eyes as he peers through the glass. 'Coming. Coming, Jim,' shouts Terry clattering down the stairs and along the bar.

'Pint a Heineken,' growling his way onto the bar stool.

'I'll get this, Patrick. Pass me a glass. I need to drain off this pump.' He pulls the handle with a firm grip. The nozzle splutters. Bubbles of froth rise. A golden liquid starts to flow. Terry stops the pump. 'Pass me that tankard over there.'

'A what?'

'That tankard. That silver mug by the sink.' Terry puts it under the nozzle and pulls the handle. He pulls it again but only halfway. A smooth cream shivers on the rim. 'There y'are now, Jim. Get that down your gullet.'

Jim flattens the cloth towel. He lays out his pipe, Virginia tobacco tin box, lighter and *The Sun*. 'Aaah,' sighing and wiping the froth from his moustache with his sleeve. Terry smiles and winks at me. I stay at the other end of the bar studying the bottle labels. I throw side-glances at Jim. Nobody speaks. The pages rustle. He slaps down each page one at a time and grunts. I think of Daddy rustling *The Derry Journal* at the kitchen table without speaking. Jim takes a pencil from his breast pocket, dampens the lead between his lips and circles items on the page. 'A fiver each way, I reckon,' mumbling. 'New?'

'Yes, I am. My first day today.'

'Irish, hey?'

'Yes.'

'I worked with Irish lads for years. Great workers and great drinkers. What's your name?'

'Patrick.'

'I mita known.'

By half past twelve there's a continuous flow of customers. According to Terry they are from the local businesses who come regularly for lunch. Some order food from the leather backed menu. Others buy a drink and crisps or peanuts. Terry picks up the telephone and presses two numbers to order the customers' choices.

'Jack Daniels, please,' asks a man in a blue, pin-striped suit.

Jack Daniels? Who's Jack Daniels?

'Pardon?' pretending not to hear.

'A Jack Daniels, please.'

'Here, take these two pints to that couple over there. I'll do the Jack Daniels,' Terry shouts.

Whiskey and lemonade on the rocks. Gin and tonic. Lager and lime. Bloody Mary. That's swearing. Whiskey and lemonade on the rocks. The only rocks I know are the ones in the field behind Crega or on the strand. The only tonic I know is the one Mammy used to give me as a child. The only lime I know are the bags Daddy scatters on the land or uses to mix concrete. A bell rings. Terry slides a cupboard door. He takes two plates of steaming food and places them at the side. He presses a red button. 'Here, take these to that couple by the window'.

I rush back wanting to see how the food comes down in the lift. The bell rings again. I slide the door and extract one plate of food. Terry points to the customer. I shut the door and press the red button. Something hums inside and then fades. 'Can you collect the glasses. We're running short of pints.'

'A Paddy whiskey!' a young man shouts. He's making fun of me. I don't like him. I'll say something to him. No. He'll laugh at my accent. He won't understand me anyway. I won't serve him again. I'll tell Terry.

By two o'clock most of the customers have gone. 'You'll be ok for a couple of minutes, won't you, Patrick? I'm going to count the takings and bag it for the bank.' I empty the slop trays, wipe the bar and tabletops, clean the ashtrays and tidy the lounge. Jim sits at the end of the bar still studying the horse-racing. He takes a slurp, wipes his lips and slides off the stool.

'See you tomorrow,' waving *The Sun* above his head.

I don't know where Hughie is. He's probably drunk in the cellar. Two ladies come in. 'Hello, two gin and tonics, please?' asks the one with the black, shoulder-length hair.

'Of course. Ice?' I look at the bottles standing on the worktop behind me. I can't see a bottle with gin written on it.

'It's up there on the optics. Gordon's Gin,' she says pointing to the upside-down bottle. I scan the bottles. I remember how Terry did it earlier. I press the glass up against the two little pieces sticking out sideways. Nothing happens. I try again. The gin spurts and stops. I hold the glass to catch the dribble. I hope they say yes. I want to lift the cubes out of the bucket with the tongs.

'Just in one, please.' I smile to myself. I drop two cubes in. They crackle and stick together.

'Not seen ye here before,' says the plumper lady. That's not a London accent. Where's she from I wonder.

'I'm new. Just started this morning.'

'Oh, a wee touch of the Irish brogue, hey.'

'Yes. You're not from London, are you? You sound Irish as well.'

'Yea. Kells. We've been here ten years and still have the twang.'

'I'm from Donegal myself.'

'Donegal. Well, I never. Our Mammy's from Buncrana. You know it?'

'A wee bit.'

'You might know her. Rose Doherty. She's a wee shop on Main Street next to Doherty's Bar.'

'Can't say, I do.'

They order another drink. I want to continue talking but I don't want Terry to catch me standing around. I wash and dry the glasses. I stand the pint glasses upside down on white table clothes. I hang the wine glasses from the rack overhead. He comes in the front door, carrying the empty white bank bag under his arm. 'Everything ok?'

'Yes, Thanks. Just tidying up.'

'Good man. Don't forget the floor at three o'clock,' pointing to the mop and bucket in the corner.

The ice tinkles as it slides against the ladies' lips. They sip the last drop. They sling their handbags over their shoulders and shuffle off the bar stools. 'We'll pop in later in the week,' says the taller lady flicking her hair over her shoulder.

'I look forward to it.'

It's 2.55pm. The hum of the fridge disturbs the silence. Terry turns off the lights and locks the door. I lie down on the red upholstered seat along the lounge wall with my coat rolled up under my head. My feet ache. Prices and names of drinks, pouring Guinness, food orders, tankards and optics flood my mind. My body goes cold. I wonder if there's a blanket anywhere. I tuck my legs in and stretch the coat over myself. I think of the taller sister's flowing black hair, her wide smile and dark eyes. I try to remember their colour but can't. I'll have to check next time. I fancy her. I wouldn't cheat on Rita at home. I promised I'd be back at the end of August. I must remember to ask the ladies their names. I'll have to tell them mine. I can't wait to see them. The chill creeps through my bones. Almost three hours before opening time. I don't want to do this every day. I want to go home. No-one told me how tired I would be. It'll be midnight by the time I get back to the flat.

Footsteps shuffle on the linoleum behind the bar. Bottles begin to tinkle. I sit up but can't see anyone. A spluttering cough. Something grates on the floor. I stand up. Hughie's bald patch bobs up and down. I tiptoe into the furthest corner and lie down on the couch behind the table. I spy on him through the table legs while he fetches crates from the cellar. Threads of smoke wriggle behind him. It's half past five. My head aches. My eyes sting. Another six hours of this. I want to go back to the flat and sleep. Oh no, the train at night. I'll get lost. I'll take the train to Holyhead in the morning and wait for the next boat. No, Kevin'll go mad.

At half past eleven I make my way to St. Paul's tube station. A black man stands by the ticket barrier. I look at him and smile. He doesn't respond. I run along the corridors. I look around. Nobody. A train thunders overhead. The tube hisses. The doors swish. A black lady and a white man sit at the far end of the row of blue and green striped cloth seats. She reads a book. She crosses her black-stockinged legs. A red handbag rests on her lap. The grey-bearded man in a long, black, overcoat and grey trousers, squashes between the arms of his seat. He scans sheets of paper through thick, black-rimmed spectacles resting on the edge of his nose.

The rope grips dangling from the ceiling sway in time with the rocking carriage as it echoes through the tunnel. The lights become brighter and flash faster. The train stops at Chancery Lane, opens and shuts doors. The man and lady don't move. Nobody gets on. I rush up to the street. A taxi waits by the exit. A lorry stands at the traffic lights. A man leads his dog along the footpath. I pace towards the flat, throwing side-glances towards the slightest sound. I sigh when I lock the door. The light from the streetlamps fills my bedroom.

On my days off I take the tube to my brother Kevin in South Ruislip. I write letters home and to Rita. On Saturday morning I go to the market. I see potatoes in plastic bags and milk in glass bottles with a silver lid.

'Great to hear from you. We were just talking about you. How's the digs?' Mammy says when she picks up the phone.

'They're ok, just a bit cramped. They're upstairs but it'll do for the summer.'

'Hope you're managing to get the hang of things in the restaurant?' Kevin must've told her I was working in a restaurant. She wouldn't let me work in a pub. If I tell her she'll force me to leave. She'll tell Daddy.

'It's ok. Always busy but the manager's good. He's from Dublin I think.'

'Oh, even better. Daddy's here if you'd like to say hello.' I don't reply. His footsteps shuffle. The phone crackles.

'Hello.'

'Hello.'

'Well, what's the weather lake over there?'

'It's ok. I'm indoors all the time so I don't see much of it.'

'You seen Kevin lately?'

'Yes. I go to his house on Saturdays when I'm off work.'

'Ok, then, ring agen when ye hev time.'

When it's quiet Terry leaves me alone more and more. I don't serve slops. I don't like serving the cheap whiskey. I like it when customers ask for an Irish coffee. 'Waw! How d'you do that? What's the secret?' I smile and tap the side of my nose. 'Where did you learn that?'

'Well, it's just coffee, sugar, whiskey, hot water and cream on top and that's it.'

After a couple of weeks I know the regulars and their drinks. Some are so punctual I can predict when they'll appear. If the bar is busy we wink at each other. I prepare the drinks and pass them with a sly move, knowing that most of them will tip well. Katie and Lizzy come most days about two o'clock. When it's quiet I chat to them as long as Terry isn't around. I fancy Katie but haven't the courage to ask her out. I know she fancies me too. A lady comes in by herself about seven o'clock and sits at the bar. We chat freely. She's drunk by nine. I ask her for a date. I meet her in Mooney's Bar on Saturday evening. We have a quick drink and agree to go somewhere else. As we pass Charing Cross she says she's just going check the time of her last train. I wait for half an hour. She doesn't return. I head back to the flat.

On my last day Terry suggests I have a drink with him after closing. I encourage the two sisters to stay. 'Well, what's it to be, Patrick?'

'Oh, just a shandy,' as I lock the door and dim the lights. I arrange the stools in a straight line against the bar and sit beside Katie. She smiles and taps me on the back. This is a good sign, I think. I tap her shoulder.

'Ah away with ye now. Have a decent drop.'

'Maybe a Guinness, then.' Terry pours a pint of Guinness and lets it settle on the bar. 'Right, girls. The usual I suppose.'

Kate and Lizzie nod. Terry places the Guinness and four gin and tonics with ice in front of us. 'Good health and good luck to ye, Patrick,' raising and sipping his gin and tonic. We clink glasses and sip. I drink half of the Guinness and finish the gin. 'The same again?'

'Yes. Just gin. No Guinness for me.' Terry places four more gins on the bar. I pass him a pound note.

'Ah, put that away for God's sake.'

I start to sing:

  I've just dropped in to see you all I'll only stay awhile
I want to hear how you're getting on
I want to hear you smile
I'm happy to be back again
And greet you big and small
For there's no place on earth just like
The homes of Donegal.

I stagger to the toilets. The urinal sways. The sink floats. The floor rises and falls. I open the door. I bump into the toilet bowl. The outline of Terry, Kate and Lizzie becomes clearer as I scramble onto the stool. Kate supports me under my arm and pecks me on the cheeks. I return the gesture. Kate and I kiss and hold hands until the early hours.

My head hurts so much at six o'clock I can't get off the lounge couch. The lights reflecting in the mirrors force me to close my eyes. I slide along the couch towards the toilet door. The tables and chairs sway. I stand up. I vomit.

'Jesus Christ, Patrick, what a mess you're in,' Terry says from the bar. 'You know how much you drank last night?'

'No.'

'Twenty-one friggen gins. A friggen bottle.' I slide back on the couch and sleep for two more hours. I sneak out the door and slouch on a windowsill outside the pub.

The Corphouse

I stood in the sitting room doorway not knowing where or who to look at. A row of chairs and two settees lined three walls of the sitting room. Not a chair was vacant, not a man in sight. My mother was sitting on a cushion-covered stool by the open fire staring at the flames. She threaded her rosary beads between her fingers stopping to caress each bead as if encouraging it to speak. 'There's a wee fella here to see ye, Lizzie,' says a voice from somewhere in the room. She raised her head in slow motion as if it was being cranked up. She squinted so hard I could barely see her eyes.

'What did you say?' her voice trembling, her hands shaking. She rubbed her eyes with the scrunched-up tissue on her lap. She leaned forward. I stepped forward. Her cheeks twitched. She had a tic that showed when she was upset. The dimples I used to see when she laughed weren't there.

'Oh my God. It's Patrick,' she whispered grabbing my arm with both of her hands. It was the first time I'd seen her without her light brown wig. The wig she wore to bingo, to the doctor's, to mass, in town and even to the hairdressers. Her dark brown slacks, the same slacks she used to wear around the house but would whip off at the sight of a visitor, were misshapen and puckered at the knees. Thick beige elasticated socks supported her swollen ankles. Her hands shook. She failed in her struggle to stand up. She smiled with embarrassment. I leaned forward and put my arm around her neck. She hid her face in my shoulder. She whimpered. She said something but I couldn't make out what. A tear trickled down my cheek. It tickled my nose. I straightened up. We looked at each other. We smiled and wiped the damp from our faces.

'Twas a heart attack, you know. In the car just outside Malin Town. I was in the front and Mary Anne Logue in the back. I'm aching from head to toe. Oh, God. Your poor Daddy'.

I turned towards my father's coffin sitting on a wheeled silver frame behind the door. I stood still and stared at his corpse dressed in his brown suit, white shirt, brown tie. I wanted to shout something but didn't know what. Dark bruises marked his forehead and nose. I wished I'd done that. I always wanted to hit him. I looked back at Mammy. She stared at her Rosary beads.

The last time I saw him dressed like this was when he used to go to the local dance hall with Mammy. The only thing missing now was the tweed hat that used to cover his few grey strands of hair flattened left to right. I wanted to cry but couldn't. This well-dressed man, whose dancing once attracted the admiration of the neighbours, disgusted me.

His face was still as stone, hard fists not softened by the rosary beads woven between his fingers. Whoever shut the eyelids when he breathed his last did me a favour. His piercing blue, chilling eyes, herring eyes I'd always thought, won't reach me anymore. I gripped my fists in my trouser pockets.

I should pick up the cards standing on the coffin. I should read them. I should bend over his face. I should kiss his forehead. I should stroke his cheek. I should make the sign of the cross. Mammy's gaze followed me. She'll be angry. She won't say anything now but she'll feel the shame. I should do it but I can't. Even for her.

I looked at Granddad's photograph above the coffin. His fist resting on his cheek looked like my father's. He had the same blue eyes. The gold paint on the thick frame had faded. It was cracked by the wood joint in one corner. Would Mammy hang a picture of my father on the wall next to him?

A row of mismatching chairs along the walls provided what comfort they could for the mourners. 'Hello, Patrick,' a voice emerged from somewhere. I looked around. A hand waved above the sea of faces. It was Cahir.

'Hello, young man. God, I haven't seen you for at least a couple of years.' He stood up and we hugged.

'Listen, I need to clarify things for the morning. Fr. Campbell's saying Mass. He was here yesterday talking about it.' I stared at Cahir. I looked away, rubbing my fingers against my chin. I feel an old rage. What was he doing agreeing to Fr. Campbell saying mass? Even Mammy didn't like him. Maybe he didn't know.

I walked into the barn where I used to hide. The blue Ford Dexta I drove to the shore for slat mara, and to Glentogher for turf, stood in the corner. A headlamp dangled from a wire. An old blanket covered the engine. My father's turf spade hung on the same peg on the wall. I made my way to the end of the lane. The sheep netting around the spring well was gone. Tall rushes covered it. I used to carry buckets of water to the kitchen from the well.

The sun began to sink behind the white gable of Mary Anne's shop. The Homes Field, being used as a carpark, was now nearly empty. I had told Mary Anne that my father had died. As a joke.

I waited for him to appear at the door. I was still scared. His absence was present. I wanted him dead. I shouldn't have been thinking like that. I wanted him alive too.

Teacher Training

I follow the students to the main door of De La Salle College, waiting for it to be unlocked. No girls. Some of the boys talk and laugh. Some look around as if trying to find someone to speak to or recognise. Some stand and stare at their feet. I stand in the middle of the queue peeping over heads to see if the glass door is open. Men and women rush around inside carrying folders, posters, and packets. They pin sheets to the blue noticeboards. They set out a long row of tables down the middle of the room and place books and papers on them. They push armchairs to the side. At nine o'clock the door lock clicks. The queue moves forward.

I wander around the stalls. Signs for the student union, football, rugby, basketball, debating, discos, library, bank and Sedgely Park College cover the noticeboards. I need to go to the bank to get my grant. That's what one of my letters said. It should have arrived from the Inner London Education Authority because I had to give my Holburn address when I applied. I hope it's here. I've only got £5 left. ILEA told me the £50 grant would be in the bank when I arrived at college. I have to buy books on my reading list, pay for the bus back to Fernholme every day and buy chocolate and milk. I won't get any more money until January.

'Your name please.'
'Patrick Doherty.'
'What's your hall of residence?'
'Fernholme.'
'Patrick Doherty. Sign here, please,' handing me a sheet of paper. I move away. I rip it open. Fifty pounds. Not a week's wage from Mooney's Bar.

'Can everyone move into the lecture hall please,' shouts a voice. I look round. Brother Austin stands at the double doors into the lecture theatre. We go in. A man in a dark suit, white shirt and blue tie stands at the front with his hands behind his back. People speak in a whisper. They stop. He stares. He waits.

He's not got a soutane on. He tells us he's Brother Albert. He begins. He goes through the history of De La Salle College. Teacher training facilities. Departments. Subjects. Attendance. Assignments. Behaviour. He explains that we have to enrol for our subject specialisms and obtain timetables in the dining room from eleven o'clock.

It's ten thirty. I walk towards the gymnasium. I look through the window. I'll be doing gymnastics here. I can't wait to meet the lecturers. The most exciting part of college life is P.E. We never did P.E at the college. The weights remind me of lifting the fifty-six pounds weights from the weigh bridge above my head in the barn at home. The rough metal of the handles used to skin my knuckles. I lifted bales of hay and saw how far I could carry them or a bag of potatoes across my shoulders. When we carted rocks from the shore, for draining the Moss Field, I lifted the heaviest rocks I could find, raised them to my chest and pushed them onto the trailer. I know I'm strong. I want to compete with the other students.

Sheila

'Kevin, the machine's stopped,' I shout.

He rushes over. Bang! The light goes red. The machine hisses. The lid flies off. Customers jump. They stare.

'Fucking hell. You didn't turn the water on.'

I bend over to check the silver knob. I start to turn it.

'Don't. You'll burn yourself.'

I pull my hand away. My fingers sting. I run to the cold tap. Kevin follows. 'Show me your hand.' Red blotches appear on my thumb and index finger. 'That's the last time you'll start the coffee machine. You could've blown the shop up, for Christ's sake.'

In September I leave Kevin, the fish and chip shop and London, and move into Parkside halls of residence on campus for my second year. No more minibus. Walk to the dining room for breakfast. Pop back to my room between lectures. Sit in the lounges and have coffee. Watch television. Meet students and staff. Sit on the garden benches. Walk along the tree lined paths. If only I could've moved in here when I first arrived I might've had a better start. I'm surprised I've lasted this long.

I blu-tack a poster almost floor to ceiling height of my idol, Rod Stewart. I set up the stereo deck I bought second hand from a student and play Rod's cassette tapes.

I spend most of the Spring term on my second teaching practice at a primary school in Burnley. It's built of blackened stone in the countryside. A coach leaves De La Salle foyer at a quarter past seven. The Irish driver hurtles along country lanes, rough roads and steep hills. He shouts 'gee up' at the coach as he holds the steering wheel with both hands, leans over it and bobs up and down like a jockey. He slaps his thigh pretending to whip his horse.

The coach drops me at a quarter past eight. I print off my worksheets on the duplicator, write my activities on the blackboard and blu-tack my visual aids on the walls. By a quarter to nine I go to the staffroom and have a cup of tea. The children don't understand everything I say and I don't understand everything they say. Mrs. Henderson, the class teacher, calls the register every morning. The children sit in silence with their arms crossed. During playtime on my second day she tells me to write the letter F differently. She doesn't like my Irish 'F'. She shows me on the blackboard and tells me not to do it anymore.

When I arrive back at Parkside I head to the dining hall before it shuts at six o'clock. Everyone laughs and shouts with relief that another week of teaching practice is over. At seven o'clock I head to Lecture Theatre 1 to watch an Irish folk group. A coach full of girls arrives from Sedgley Park College of Education for the disco. De La Salle nicknames them the *rent-a-crowd*. Some shout to the De La Salle Students and wave. Northern Ireland accents seem to fill the theatre. We sing. We clap. We stand and wave our arms. When the concert is finished they head to the student union bar. I return to my room. I take a quick shower, trim my moustache and curl my hair so that the ends curl inwards around my jaw. I pull on my black t-shirt, green flared trousers and black platform shoes. I push my pipe, tin box of Virginia tobacco and lighter into my two pockets. They bulge. I head to the student union bar. Girls throng the corridor, the cloakroom and toilet doorways. Donal from Enniskillen stands by a small table at the disco door. 'You want to buy a ticket, Patrick? It's for the cause,' he shouts. I shake my head and head down the steps to the bar. Girls huddle. I squeeze forward.

'A pint of Guinness, please,' I shout over their heads.

I stretch my neck to make sure the barman doesn't slip in any slops from the tray. Its frothy head isn't as good as the one I used to pull in Mooney's Bar. I sidle to the window and rest my drink on the ledge beside my pipe and tobacco. I fill the pipe halfway making sure I don't press the tobacco too hard. With one hand under the pipe, I click the lighter and turn it sideways with the other. Flames make the threads of tobacco curl. I breathe in hard until the tobacco turns red. Once lit, I tilt my head and puff the smoke towards the ceiling.

By eleven o'clock there's standing room only. A haze of cigarette smoke clouds the lights. I squint. I manage to stand up by holding onto the bar stools. 'Another Guinness, please.' The barman screws up his face, his hand to his ear. 'Another Guinness, please,' I shout holding my glass over heads and pointing to it. He smiles and gives me the thumbs up.

'Hello,' a red-haired girl says as I turn away.

'Hello.'

I rest my backside against the ledge. I light my pipe again. The girl waves. I wave back. She approaches. She flicks back her hair. It ripples down her back to her waist. I look at the half pint glass of purple liquid. 'You look like Barry Sheene. Has anyone ever told you?'

'Who's Barry Sheene?'

'You know. The motorbike racing driver.'

'Not really. What that's you're drinking?'

'Lager and blackcurrant.'

'Sounds horrible.' We stand. We look around. We smile. I sway. She grabs my Guinness and puts it on the ledge. My head slouches. She pushes my shoulders against the wall.

'You've had enough, I think.'

'What's your name?'

'Sheila.'

'I'm Patrick,' trying to shake her hand. 'You're English. Where you from?'

'Shipley,'

'Where's that?'

'Yorkshire near Bradford. I never say I'm from Bradford 'cos Shipley's posher.'

'I'm from Malin Head.'

'Where?'

'Malin Head' I explain about Northern Ireland and the border. I explain about County Donegal and Malin Head. She nods and smiles. She kisses my cheeks. I kiss her lips. She squeezes my hand. We cuddle.

'Hiya. I'm Fiona. I'm Sheila's friend. We have to get the coach in ten minutes. Why don't you come to Sedgley next weekend for the disco? I'm on the social committee. I'll make sure you get in.'

'Well, I'll see.' They head off. Sheila waves back. They go up the steps. They wobble. I shuffle through the crowd onto the corridor. I grapple my way along the walls. My head spins.

'You're a bit the worse for wear, aren't you?' a voice shouts from the toilet door. 'Bloody Donegal men. They've no sense!' I straighten myself up. My body tenses. My fists clench. I stare at him. I lunge at him. I grab his shirt collar and push him against the wall. I push hard. 'Sorry, it's only a joke.'

'Don't you ever fucking say again I've no sense.' I release my grip and wobble out.

The Star of the Sea

The ladies had finished in the kitchen. The row of chairs in the sitting room was empty. Mum wasn't there. Kevin and John were sitting by the fire. They forced a smile. 'You need to go to bed. You've been travelling all day,' Kevin said. 'I'm happy to stay here all night. I never sleep much anyway.'

'I'll stay a while and see how I go on.' We sat. We stared out the windows at the darkness descending. We looked at the coffin. We looked at each other. My throat was dry. My coughs disturbed the silence. I wanted to speak but didn't know what to say. I knew they wanted to speak too. When did I last see John and Kevin? When did we last talk? What were they thinking?

'You heard that story about the men carrying the coffin and going to Farren's Bar?' John asked.

'No.'

'The Houghtons, who lived up past the chapel, used to make coffins many years ago. Somebody died so four of the family went to Houghtons to collect a coffin. On the way home with the coffin they went into Farren's Bar and left the coffin outside the door. After a few drinks a neighbour snuck into the coffin and pulled the lid down to get a lift to his house. Later in the evening the four men were so drunk they didn't notice that the coffin was heavier. They carried it home.'

'What happened?'

'Nobody knows.'

I gave a quiet laugh. I stared at the wooden flowerpot stands by each window. I had cut out the circular tops and bases and sanded the strips of thin wood long enough for the tops to slip under the window ledge. I think I had got the idea from one of John's carpentry books. I couldn't remember how I managed to make them in the barn without my father catching me. All I remember was peeping through the barn window every few minutes to make sure he wasn't coming and hiding everything under old sacks if I heard his footsteps. Where did I get the wood and screws from? Perhaps I got them from John's wood store. Where did I get the wood stain from? What did Mummy say when I gave her the stands? I don't remember my father saying anything to me about them. I wonder if Mum told him.

I drew the curtains and turned on the light. The two candles on the sideboard at the end of the coffin had burned down almost to the brass base. Hardened wax coated the lip. I blew them out. Next to them stood a black and white A3 photograph resting against a vase. It was a married couple. Its edges were frayed and turned inwards. I held it at arms' length to take in the detail. A lady sat erect on a cushion covered stool. Her feet overlapped and retracted underneath. Her hands rested on the expensive-looking tweed skirt. The matching jacket and wide-rimmed tilted hat adorned with a long feather emphasised her elegance. The black-framed spectacles highlighted her haughty expression. A gentleman dressed in a dark two-piece suit, white shirt and dark tie stood to her right. His left leg, bent, rested on a ledge. His hands, the right over the left, capped his left knee. His piercing eyes and full head of neatly combed black hair highlighted his handsome appearance.

'Who's this?'

'It's Mammy and Daddy's wedding photo from 1937. Theresa found it yesterday when she was clearing out Daddy's stuff.'

'Never! I wouldn't know it's them.' I turned towards the coffin. Only a few flattened grey strands of hair remained. His face was podgy. Thin red lines zigzagged over his cheeks. I couldn't work out whether these were the result of the car accident or whether they were caused by a lifetime of exposure to the elements or daily shaving. Loose skin hung under his chin. I thought of how Mum looked now. Her face was wrinkled. Her cheeks sunken. Her earlobes drooped. A vacant look in her eyes. Her wedding ring had sunk into her finger.

I turned the photo over. The white backing was brown near the edges. I turned it back again. I stared at it. It must have been lying there for years. I wondered whether Mum had hidden it. She used to hint that she had wanted to be a nun but in those days a local woman married a local man and had children. The husband worked the land and the wife was a domestic servant within her own home. Further education and careers weren't an option. She was trapped in a world she didn't choose. Where could I get a copy of it?

John and Kevin rested their heads on the back of the armchairs. Their eyes closed and opened. They shuffled. I tiptoed to the bedroom where I used to sleep as a boy. I shivered. The table where I did my homework was gone. The fireplace was empty. The coal bucket was empty. A fusty smell filled the room. I slipped my shoes off. I wound up the cream alarm clock with the two bells on top of the dressing table and set the time. Its tick tock seemed louder now. I flicked the switch on the door frame. I groped my way to the bed. I wanted to flip back the eiderdown. I didn't. I lay on it. I sniffed the pillow. Cold air circled my head. I tossed and turned through the night checking the illuminated hands on the clock.

At ten o'clock the undertakers arrived to get the coffin to the funeral mass at eleven. The chief undertaker announced to the room that the coffin would close in fifteen minutes. A queue began to form at the door. Mourners filed along the side of the coffin, stopped near the middle, making a quick sign of the cross, giving a sudden jerk of the knee and mumbled. They turned away, shook hands with each of us and bowed their heads. The men made their way outside. The women held rosary beads and caressed my father's head. They kissed his forehead. When the last one had left the room, the door closed. We watched in silence as the undertakers removed the cards from the coffin, lifted the lid resting against the wall near my father's head and placed it on top. They pushed golden screws into the slots and tightened them with a small tool.

No-one shed a tear. We looked at each other in silence. He's trapped inside. He'll never escape. Safe from the herring-blue eyes, his giant calloused right hand and the shuffling shoes. Mum tottered forward supported by Cahir. The last time I saw her standing she was taller. Her shoulders reached the edge of the coffin that rested on the silver legs with wheels attached. She rubbed her hand back and forth along the lid as if telling it to lift. Her shoulders trembled. She bowed her head. With a final gentle tap she turned away, gazing at each of us without speaking. A tear escaped from behind her glasses. The undertakers signalled with their hands that the coffin was ready to be lifted. My brother James organised the brothers into pairs according to height: James at the front, Kevin and John, Brendan and Willie and Cahir and myself. With one undertaker at each end and three brothers on each side we hoisted the coffin holding the six-foot corpse onto our shoulders with shaking arms. We linked arms. James led the procession out the front door, down the cement path and along the lane to the hearse waiting on the road. My sister Theresa and Mum linked arms and followed behind. A young, assistant undertaker gathered the wreaths and placed them in the hearse.

We followed the coffin in a hearse to The Star of The Sea Chapel in. We knelt down, stared and waited. I thought of Dan's funeral. Dan, the brother above me, had died at twenty-seven. It was the only time I saw my father cry. He shouted at his coffin as it was being loaded into the hearse. I looked at my father's coffin now standing in front of the altar. I imagined him falling out of the coffin with a tear trickling along his nose. I imagined his outstretched knotted twig fingers covered in cracked bark-like skin and eagle-hooked claws, begging to touch me.

Cahir's daughters started to play their guitars. Everybody stood. They began to sing. The brown sacristy door creaked. Three altar boys processed around the bottom step followed by Father Campbell. The last time I saw him was twenty years ago at school. They took up their positions by the side of the altar. He opened a book on the lectern. The strands of grey hair still lay flat across his bald head but his stomach protruded more. Perhaps it was the white vestments that exaggerated his girth. He concentrated on his book. He looked up at everyone. Silence. Were the leather strap or his curved pipe were still in his deep pocket? I wished I had known at school that the correct term for his pipe was *the bent bulldog*. He spoke in his familiar, quiet, but nonchalant tone. My hands began to perspire. My face burnt. I couldn't look at him. I couldn't go to Holy Communion and be close to him again. My family was confused as they squeezed past me in the pew on their way to the altar. Since when did Patrick not go to Holy Communion? Father Campbell raised his eyes to the ceiling in adoration of The Blessed Sacrament. He looked meekly in the communicants' eyes.

'Corpus Christi.'
'Amen.'

At the end of mass father Campbell descended the two marble steps. The flab under his chin was wobblier now and half covered his collar. Brown spots partially speckled the backs of his hands, hidden by the loose vestment sleeves. The two altar boys, stern and rigid, stood at either side of him. Without speaking, he faced one of them and held out his hand. The altar boy passed him a prayer book. After reading a prayer he pushed it into the boy's chest. He stared at the second altar boy, holding the bowl of incense and thurible, held out his hand, and took a spoonful. He tapped it into the thurible receptacle.

Smoke rose. Holding the thurible chain at shoulder height, he swayed the receptacle over the coffin. I thought of how he used to swing the leather strap. Did he hit the altar boys in the presbytery?

À Harfleur

'Excusez-moi, Monsieur. Est-ce qu'il y a un bus à Gonfreville l'Orcher ?' I say to the bus driver. I've come by ferry to Le Havre. I'm worried about being understood.

'Non. Il n'y a plus d'autobus ce soir. Le prochain est le matin à huit heures.'

'Gonfreville l'Orcher, c'est loin d'ici ?'

'Environ six kilomètres.'

'Pardon ?'

'Six kilomètres, peu près.' Oh, I thought.

'Est-ce qu'il y a un hôtel par ici ?'

'Oui, sur Route d'Orcher. Deux ou trois kilomètres d'ici. Il faut suivre la route tout droit là-bas.'

I pick up my case and walk along the streets. I cross the bridge over La Riviere Lezarde and continue until I see Route l'Orcher. After about a quarter of a mile a sign points to Gonfreville l'Orcher. I follow the road for half a mile. It branches off to the left. It's getting dark. My arms ache. My legs hurt. I'm hungry. No traffic. No houses. Silence. The silhouette of the top of a factory building in the distance attracts my attention. The smell of sea fills the air. I sit on my case. I want to go back to Harfleur and get the next bus to Le Havre. I start walking again, swapping my case from hand to hand. I turn a corner. A light shines in the distance. I feel relieved. I quicken my step. Through the window I see a group of men standing by the bar. I open the door and sidle in with my case. Everyone stops and looks. 'Bonsoir, Monsieur. Vous voulez quelque chose à boire ? Asks the barman.

'Non, merci Monsieur. Vous avez une chambre pour ce soir ?'

'Non. Je ne crois pas.'

'Je suis perdu. Je veux aller à Gonfreville l'Orcher. Je suis 'l'assistant d'anglais.'

'Attendez. Je parle avec ma femme.' He heads into the back. I stand. I smile nervously. I want to say something.

'Madame vous trouvera une chambre. Elle est sympa,' says a man at the end of the bar. I think he said his wife would find me a room. I'm so exhausted I'll sleep anywhere. Madame comes into the bar followed by the barman. She smiles but doesn't speak. She beckons me to follow her. A single black metal frame bed with spots of rusk stands by the dirty white window. A thick blanket is folded back halfway.

'Voilà,' she says pointing to the bed.

'Merci,' nodding in response.

'Le petit déjeuner est à huit heures.'

'Merci.' I shut the door as she leaves. I drag what's left of the dishevelled curtain and flop onto the mattress. It squeaks. It sags in the middle. The voices downstairs begin to fade. I turn off the light. The switch seems upside down. It's so dark I can't see my hand. The lumpy bolster and uneven mattress make me toss and turn. My neck begins to ache.

As dawn begins to arrive a few cars pass by. Fields of neglected grass extend towards the tall building. Lights shine. Car brake lights glow as they turn into it. A door rattles downstairs. The voices of the owners raise and lower as they move around. Glasses clatter. Something scrapes along the floor. I pack my case. I can hardly lift it. I don't know if I have the energy to walk for another hour. I stumble downstairs, resting the case on each step.

'Bonjour, Monsieur. Petit déjeuner ?'

'Bonjour, Monsieur. Oui, s'il vous plaît.'

'C'est là,' as he points to the small square table in the corner. He places a white plate with one croissant on it. He rests a wide cup of hot chocolate beside it. He smiles. 'Voilà, Monsieur,' nodding and smiling.

'Merci, Monsieur.' I stare at the table. He must be bringing more. There must be cereal, bread and jam. I watch him rushing around behind the bar. Perhaps he's waiting for me to finish the croissant and chocolate. I gulp everything. I sit and wait.

'Vous avez terminé ?' he calls from the bar.

'Oui.' He gathers the items from the table. I wait. He looks. We smile at each other. I look out the window at the cars passing. 'Est-ce qu'il y a un taxi ou un autobus par ici ?'

'Non, Rien. Il faut téléphoner Harfleur mais c'est trop tôt. Vous allez à Gonfreville ?'

'Oui, Je vais au Collège d'Enseignment Secondaire, Gustave Courbet.'

'O là, là. C'est trois kilomètres.'

I pay for the bed and breakfast. And set off along Route l'Orcher again. I climb the long, winding road to Gonfrevillle L'Orcher. eventually I turn left at La Mairie. A sign reads *Collège d'Enseignement Secondaire, Gustave Courbet* in white. Lights shine from a balcony on the first floor of the two-storey block. I ring the bell to the right of the glass door. Two desks at right angles are strewn with papers and folders. The shelves can't hold anymore textbooks. Footsteps clatter on the cement steps.

'Bonjour, Monsieur. Je cherche Monsieur Leroux,' I say, my voice shaking.

'Oui, c'est moi,' looking over his silver framed glasses.

'Je m'appelle Patrick Doherty. Je suis l'assistant anglais.'

'Ah, Patrick. Bienvenu à Gonfreville.' I stare up at his thick grey beard and full head of wavy grey hair. He extends his hand. I shake it. He squeezes firmly. I remember someone telling me that a firm handshake is a good sign. I take a deep breath. I don't know what to say next. I smile.

'Je vous montre votre chambre. Entrez. C'est au premier étage,' I follow him up the winding steps. He continues to talk but I can't understand everything. We walk along the landing. He says the names on the three doors. He opens the door at the end with no name. 'Voilà votre chambre.'

A window faces me. I step in. A door to my left leads to the toilet and sinks. The head of the bed touches the toilet wall. There's a small gap between the end and the square table. A bolster with a clean cover lies near two white folded sheets and a yellow blanket. A fold-up wooden chair is pushed underneath the table. A single electric round socket with two small holes is embedded into the corner of the wall at table height. 'Si vous avez besoin de quelque chose, n'hésitez pas à demander.'

'Merci Monsieur.' He closes the door. I sit on the bed.

It's Sunday tomorrow. No food. No tea. No coffee. I ask Monsieur Leroux about a cooker and cooking items. He gives me a small camping stove, a saucepan and a frying pan. I go the supermarket and scour the shelves. I decide to buy things based on the pictures.

On Sunday evening I realise my clothes need ironing for the morning. I clear the table, lay a towel down and stretch out my black trousers. I lay another towel on top. I warm the frying pad. I move it back and forth making sure it doesn't burn. I reheat the frying pan. The creases disappear. A straight line runs down the front of the trousers. I repeat the routine with my white shirt. It looks good.

I head to the staffroom at eight o'clock. I stand at the back. Monsieur Leroux distributes papers. He introduces me. I'm not sure what he says. He points to a lady. I assume I'm to go with her. I smile at her and nod. The bell rings. She signals. 'Je m'appelle Danielle Durand. Vous travaillez avec moi,' shaking my hand with a firm grip.

'Bonjour, Danielle.' I'm not sure whether to kiss her on both cheeks or not. I don't know which cheek to kiss first. I'll watch what others do. I follow her.

Throughout the day classes come to her room. She leads them through the English activities in the textbook, plays tapes which the pupils repeat and practise in twos. I move around the tables, helping with the pronunciation. As the weeks progress I take small groups for reading, writing, speaking and listening activities. I end up taking *la sixième classe* once a week.

Freddie, who can't concentrate or behave properly shouts: 'Regarde l'ongle !' I realise he's telling everyone to look at the fingernail that was caught in the two cogs when I was four years old. I have learned over the years to tuck my finger into my palm. I feel my face getting hot. I tuck it well in. I refuse to show it. 'Salot,' I say under my breath, not realising some heard me. 'Il a dit *salot !'* Freddie calls out. Everybody laughs. I can't stop them. I can't continue. I ask a pupil to go and find Danielle. I explain as best I can in French. She takes Freddie.

Later in the term I teach a final year class to sing Rod Stewart's *Only a Hobo*. I hand out copies of the lyrics. The pupils repeat each line after me. I read each verse. They repeat the verse. I play the tape. Everyone listens and follows the text. I play the tape again. I encourage everyone to join in:

As I was out walking on the corner one day,
I spied an old hobo, in the doorway he lay.
His face was all covered in the cold sidewalk floor.
I guess he'd been there for a whole night or more.

They like the novelty of the English song but find the words difficult to understand. I explain it in French, but it doesn't have the same appeal to the class. I realise for the first time that a direct translation doesn't always work. It's one of my favourite songs and I'm disappointed.

I look forward to the two hours lunch break at twelve and the small bottle of wine each member of staff is given. The first few times I drink it I am half drunk and sleep it off before the afternoon lessons. Sometimes I keep the wine until the evening and drink it from one of the fancy small jam jars I use as wine glasses. 'Vous voulez emprunter un cyclomoteur ? J'en ai un,' Josianne asks me one day.

'Mais oui, bien sûr, mais je n'ai pas de permis de conduire.'

'Ce n'est pas obligatoire.' The following day she brings the moped to school. I drive the six kilomètres to Harfleur during which it splutters, cuts out, refuses to speed up and wobbles. On the way back I discover that I need to pedal for longer and faster for it to work properly. After a couple of weekends, I've learned the knack of a smooth ride.

In the summer term I venture to Le Havre. I decide to go to the beach. I put on my sunglasses and strip to my waist. I lie on my front. My backside sinks into the soft sand. After an hour I turn onto my back. I turn my head from side to side. I nod off. A child screams near me. I wake with a start. My hair is wet. My skin is sweating. It begins to tingle.

As I drive back to my room my skin itches more and more. My collar rubs my neck. By the time I arrive in my room my shirt begins to stick. I look in the mirror. Two pale circles surround my eyes. My nose shines bright red. My face and neck are less red. I take off my shirt. It hurts where it's damp. I peel it off more slowly. A blanket of red covers my body. I twist to see my back. My skin twinges. I lie on a towel on the bed. I turn. I turn again and again. The sting spreads. My skin begins to tighten. I dab a damp towel over me. I take my trousers off. My legs look so white. The pain and the tightening of the skin increases during the evening. The sheets are damp. I feel sick. No matter which way I turn, my body itches. My skin stings where it creases.

In the morning I grapple my way along the edge of the bed and toilet door. A deep red covers me. I sip a glass of water. The supermarket's shut. The chemist is shut. I don't want to knock on Monsieur Leroux's door on a Sunday. The children will laugh at me in the morning. The staff will think what a fool I've been. I'll leave a note on Monsieur's door. I'll stay in bed.

I get up at seven o'clock. I need to go to school. My face and neck sting less. I try to wash and shave. I can't close my shirt collar. I leave my tie. I can't button my cuffs. I head towards the staffroom. I open the door. Everyone looks. The conversation stops. Someone mumbles something. 'Patrick, qu'est-ce que tu as fait ?' says Danielle holding her hand over her mouth. I shrug my shoulders, forgetting that the shirt would rub. Others join in. I can't make out what they're saying but I know they're concerned.

'Une autre lettre pour vous, Patrick,' says Monsieur Leroux, handing me a letter from Sheila with the UK stamp and kisses round the edges. I wait for the staff to say something about the blue kisses but they don't today. The bell rings. I follow Danielle. I pretend to rub my face as I pass the pupils. Some look. Some make comments. She enters the classroom. The pupils stare.

'Bonjour, tout le monde,' I rub my face again. 'Que je suis stupide !'

'Qu'est-ce qui s'est passé, Monsieur ?' Asks Pierre in the corner.

'Ça suffit !' Danielle replies in a firm voice.

As the morning progresses, the sunburn eases. I turn my neck from side to side waiting for the sting. By lunch time I have relaxed more. Most of the children have seen me. At the end of the day Josianne meets me in the staffroom. 'Tu veux dîner chez moi un soir ?'
    'Oui, je veux bien, Vous êtes très gentille.'
    'Vous êtes libre samedi vers huit heures ?'
    'Oui, ça va pour moi.'
    She kisses me on both cheeks. I reciprocate.

Throughout the week we bump into each other in the staffroom and corridor. We exchange pleasantries. I think about what Sheila would say if I tell her. We've been together for six months. I want to be honest, but I don't want to hurt her. If I don't tell her I'll feel guilty. Perhaps I should tell Josianne about Sheila. She must know. She'll have seen the letters. She's never said anything.

    'Bonsoir, Patrick.' She hugs me and kisses me on both cheeks.
    'Bonsoir, Josianne.'
    'Entre, suis-moi.' I follow her upstairs. I breathe in her perfume. Low music plays. The small square table is laid. A bottle of red wine is open. 'Enlève ta veste et assieds-toi.'
    'Merci bien.'
    'Tu veux un verre de vin ?' pointing to the bottle of red.
    'Un petit verre.'
    'Santé,' we say to each other, raising glasses.

    At half past nine the sun begins to sink. Josianne pulls the curtains. 'Alors, je crois que je dois partir. Je ne veux pas conduire dans le noir.'
    'Juste un peu plus de vin, Patrick ?' Josianne begins to tilt the bottle.
    'Non, j'en ai eu assez,' stretching my hand over my glass.

    As I return from the toilet I pick up my coat from the back of the couch. She sits and smiles raising her glass to her lips. I look at my glass. It's three quarters full. I pick up the keys and leave.

First Post

I move in with Sheila, in her flat in Rochdale. Her Catholic mother, from County Monaghan, and father, from County Cavan, visit us at least once a month on a Sunday afternoon. Sheila tells her I live there but never tells her father. Before they arrive we tidy the flat to clear away any evidence of me. I tell him I live on the top floor with a friend from college.

'Have you got a teaching post yet for September, Patrick?' Mr. Fagan, the head of French, asks me one day in June.
'No. Not yet. I keep looking in all the papers and applying.'
'The Headteacher of St. Gabriel's Secondary School in Bury is looking for a French teacher. Are you interested?'
'Yes.'
'I'll ring and ask him to send you an application form.'
'Thank you very much.'

I receive a letter inviting me for interview. I have to arrive at eleven o'clock to meet Mr. Banks, the Headteacher and Mr. Kenna, the Head of French who will give me a tour of the school. Then there's lunch. The interview is to start at one o'clock.

I sit on the wooden chair by Mr. Banks' door. I wait. A wooden clock ticks above the hall door. A man's voice bellows along the corridor to my right. A door slams. A boy walks past. Mr. Banks opens his door. I jump up. 'Welcome to St. Gabriel's, Mr. Doherty,' extending his hand.
'Good morning, Mr. Banks,' I say, shaking his hand.
'Mr. Kenna, the Head of French, will be along in a moment to give you a tour of the school. I'll meet you again at one o'clock for the interview upstairs in the *Quiet Room*.'

I sit and wait. It's ten past eleven. 'Hello,' says Mr. Kenna coming down the stairs in his short-sleeved, open-necked, white shirt. 'You must be Patrick.'
'Yes, I am.'
'My name is Mr. Kenna. Please call me Andy,' he says in a Liverpudlian accent. 'Let me give you a tour of the school first.' Andy leads me along different corridors on both floors, pointing out the classrooms. 'This is my classroom on the left. The other classroom is in the 210 Block.'
'Why is it called the 210 Block?'
'It was built to hold two hundred and ten first year pupils. There are seven classes of thirty. I'll show you.'

After visiting the 210 Block, Andy accompanies me to the dining hall where we have a school lunch. We have to raise our voices to hear ourselves over the pupils. We finish quickly. 'There's still half an hour before the interview. You can come to the staffroom for a coffee or have a walk around.'

'I think I'll walk around. Are there any other candidates?'

'No. You're the only one. It'll be all over by half past one. Come back to Mr. Banks' office at five to one and I'll meet you there.'

'Right, Patrick,' Andy says coming down the stairs, tapping his tie and buttoning his jacket. 'Follow me.' He opens the door with *Quiet Room* written on it. A rectangular table stands in the middle. Four men sit around it. They smile.

'Please take a seat, Patrick,' Andy says pointing to the end chair.

'Welcome, Patrick. Let me introduce everyone,' Mr. Banks says. 'This is Father Flynn. He's the chairman of the governors. This is Mr. Ireland, our school advisor. You've already met Mr. Kenna.' Everyone nods and smiles. 'You've had a look around the school this morning. What did you think of it?'

I stare at him trying to think of what to say. 'I like the library. I looked at the Longmans French textbooks and tapes the pupils used.'

'I see from your application that you've completed the Catholic Teachers' Certificate of Religious Education,' says Father Flynn. 'What did you do in the course?

'I studied the scriptures and books of teaching Religious Education. I became familiar with different schemes of work and learned how to plan lessons.'

'You've done all your teaching experiences in primary schools, I see,' says Mr. Ireland. Did you teach any French?'

'No.'

'Do you think you're confident enough to teach French in a secondary school?

'Yes. I spent a year working in a secondary school in France where I taught English.

'How would you begin to teach first year pupils?' Andy asks.

'I would start with simple phrases like *hello, goodbye, how are you? What is your name?* I would organise the pupils into groups so that they could practise. I would introduce the Present Tense of regular 'er' verbs.'

'How would you introduce the Present Tense?'

'I would have to explain what it is in English first and then demonstrate how it works in a French verb on the blackboard. I would use examples from the scheme of work.'

'Are there any questions you'd like to ask?' Asks Mr. Banks.

'No, Thank you.'

Mr. Banks explains that the governors need time to discuss the interview. He asks me to sit outside his room and wait. Silence. I'd like to work here. I'd like to join the staff five-a-side football at lunchtime that he mentioned. The clock hand moves so slowly. A door opens upstairs. I look up. Footsteps scurry along the corridor. No-one appears. Another door upstairs opens. Andy appears. 'Right, Patrick. Please come back in.'

I sit and stare. The men stare. 'Thank you for coming for the interview, Mr. Doherty,' Mr. Banks says looking over his glasses. 'We would like to offer you the post. Are you willing to accept it?'

'Yes, I am,' smiling at him.

'Mr. Ireland will talk to you about your probationary year and Mr. Kenna will sort out the practicalities for the first term.'

Lagg

I sat in the back seat of the second funeral car with Cahir, Kevin and Bredan. We didn't speak. The lines of mourners, with hands overlapping their stomachs, thinned out as we left the church. I tried to identify their faces, half-hidden by tight caps, veils and buttoned-up collars. I wondered what they knew. I looked out the rear window. A procession of cars followed us along the winding road to the cemetery at Lagg Chapel, near the Five Finger Strand.

The hearse groaned up the steep slope in front of the chapel through the black metal gates and along the graveyard wall before turning left towards the grave. The hole had been dug deep enough to accommodate mammy. Theresa linked arms with her. They wobbled over the rough grass, gripping more and more tightly, as they approached the mound. Mammy watched the coffin as it was carried from the hearse. She watched as it was lowered and slid out of sight. What was she thinking about? Father Campbell read two passages from The Bible and said some prayers before dropping a trowel full of soil on top of my father. Mammy picked up a handful of dirt, leant forward and dropped it. My brothers followed. I walked away.

Back at the house our family and neighbours sat in the sitting room drinking teas and eating sandwiches. Mum sat on her stool staring at the floor. She nibbled a triangular sandwich. Behind her in the corner stood the glass door bookcase that James had made at evening classes at my old school. I opened the Geography textbook I had used for Honours Leaving Cert. "Patrick Doherty, Grega, Malin Head, Ballygorman P.O, Lifford, County Donegal, Europe, Northern Hemisphere, World" was written in blue ink. I thought it was one of the pens I used to mess with in the blue mission's box I kept on my table. I smiled at the memory. Diagrams of volcano structure, oxbow lakes, weather symbols and river erosion reminded me of the time I had spent copying them for homework. The gold-coloured coal scuttle with its matching poker, brush and pan stood on the hearth. Matching black and white dogs still stood guard on the fireplace. The end of one ear was now chipped.

I looked out the window. The whitewashed wall was cracked. Green moss grew along the bottom. She'd have asked James to repaint it but he would've been too busy on the farm. I walked into the kitchen. It was tidier now after all the chairs had been put away. The brown-checked carpet hadn't changed apart from the faded area by the door. The three-seater settee, the armchair and television remained. The bucket of turf stood by the grate. The smell of firelighters filled the room. Strips of *The*

Farmers' Journal lay on top. The folding dining table covered with the same plain green throw-over stood by the window. The wireless sat on the corner shelf with its dial on Radio Eireann to broadcast the Angelus at midday, the news at one and the Angelus again at six. The dial didn't seem to have moved since I was here last. Mammy's soft footstool sat underneath the settee with *The Derry Journal* on it. I flicked through the pages.

   I walked through to the scullery. The row of head-height cupboards made by John in 1960 were still attached to the wall. Their lime green surface was greasy. Mum mustn't have been able to reach up to wash them anymore. She would've been too proud to ask anyone. I opened one door. Inside twelve cobwebbed dinner plates rested on ripped newspaper now brown with age. Dust and cobwebs sealed the joints between the wooden frame and the sickly yellow wall at the back of the cupboard. I pushed the door shut giving an extra heave to squeeze its misshaped frame back into place. A drawer under the worn artificial-marble worktop played host to haphazardly placed knives, forks and spoons, discoloured and spotted with age. I picked up a tablespoon and rubbed it with my thumb. I used to use *Duraglit* at weekends to polish the cutlery. I made no impression on it. The drawer rasped its way back in. I ran my hand over the chipped Belfast sink where I use to sit while Mum bathed me. A thick grey rubber pipe connected the cream Rayburn range to an orange-coloured bottle of Calor gas. An aluminium kettle sat on the large ring. I touched the handle. It was warm. My father used to sit at the green formica table behind me. He'd drink cup after cup of tea from the tin teapot sizzling on the corner of the range.

   I stared at the latch of the brown back door that used to click when he entered. I wiped my eyes. I looked upwards. The two rusting hooks that used to hold my father's jumpers and coats were bare. The head-height fridge-freezer, ultra-modern for its time, chilling the jugs of fresh cows' milk, was gone. I opened the newer waist-height one. A litre milk carton sat in the door shelf. A pack of Kerrygold butter and slices of ham wrapped in cling film rested on a shelf. The multi-coloured tea caddy with its hinged lid and patches of bare tin stood empty on the windowsill. I thought of the brown paper bag of loose tea Mary Anne used to measure out of the tea chests in her shop for Mum.

   I headed back to the sitting room. Mum was still sitting by the fire. Anne Kelly was talking to her. I wanted to go to Mum and say something but didn't know what. I tiptoed to my parents' bedroom door. I hesitated before entering. I felt I shouldn't. I felt I was intruding into Mum's sanctuary. I waited in the doorway for the smell of camphor to subside. The door was only ever opened wide enough for Mum and my father to go in and out. They'd shut it immediately. I'd hear Mum's muffled voice. Nobody else ever entered. I once slept in the single bed behind the door when I had chickenpox at eight years old. The iron double bed with its black metal headboard stood by the window. Gold-coloured balls about the size of my fist sat on top of the bedposts. I wonder who slept on which side? I looked out the window. The breeze blocks of the pump house and outside toilet wall blocked my view. I hid there. The gold-coloured framed fireplace was hidden behind a mesh screen. The air smelled of damp.

The brown wooden wardrobe stood at the side. One door was ajar. That must have been the door I used to hear Mum slamming every time she changed her clothes. A brown wooden chest of drawers with a tilting mirror hid Mum's creams and jewellery. Her brown wig lay on top. I headed back to the sitting room. I stood in the doorway. Anne Kelly was still talking to Mum. Mum nodded. I thought of when Anne had come to the house when Brendan was born, how they talked about stitches and how the nappy bucket stank when I carried it to the scullery.

I carried on to the bathroom. The pale-green suite remained the same. The sealant around the sink and bath wasn't white anymore. The smooth enamel on the bottom of the bath had worn through to the fibreglass. An aluminium chair frame straddled the bath. Why didn't someone tell me she was so fragile, so restricted in her movement. How did she enter and exit the bath without falling? I knew my father wouldn't have helped her. I don't ever remember him using the bathroom. He preferred to wash himself in the boiler house by the kitchen.

The cream perished rubber hose of the showerhead curled around the taps. I forced one tap so hard that my knuckles turned white and my palm stung. A gurgle erupted in the bowels of the underfloor plumbing, reverberating more and more loudly. The water approached. I waited. Spits and splutters belched into the bath and trickled down the plughole. I tried the other tap. I couldn't open it. I pulled the long grubby cord to test the light. It worked. I pulled the cord again. I tried to close the door behind me. It stuck on the metal strip on the floor.

'I'm going for a lie down, Patrick.' I jumped round. Mum tottered to her bedroom. She shut the door. I walked down the hallway towards my bedroom. The floorboards creaked in the same places. The cream lampshade had gone brown. The weak bulb did little to light up the brown carpet on the narrow passageway. I sat on the eiderdown. It still smelt damp. I stared at the empty fireplace.

'Gosh, you've been studying hard, Patrick. You must be exhausted,' Mammy used to say when I'd go to the kitchen at nine o'clock for my supper of milk, bread and jam.

I shut the door as I left. I headed down the hallway to the 'end room'. It had always been called the 'end room' because it was added onto the end of the house when I was about ten years old. Tom Bann who lived on the mountain road built it. He liked to catch me and rub his stubble on my face. It hurt. He'd joke about putting me under the floor joists. I'd run.

I looked out the window. I thought of the day Cahir arrived home from the priesthood. Mammy would have longed for Cahir to lead the funeral Mass. The smell of fresh floorboards and melted tar on the flat roof rushed back to me. A chill still filled the room. Both beds were in the same place they had always been. One for Dan and one for me. James slept in the other one for a while. I couldn't remember where he slept afterwards. Mammy slept in the second bed during the spring and autumn when my father went to Scotland to work on the farms. I had pretended to be asleep while she cried. When he went for the boat he left without saying goodbye.

First Day

I am in the foyer at a quarter past eight. My first day. A cement spiral staircase winds overhead out of sight. Halfway up *Staffroom* in blue capitals, on a wooden rectangle, hangs on the cream wall. Muffled voices upstairs disturb the quiet. I lean over the curled end of the metal banister and stretch my neck. I can't see anyone. I hear footsteps. A hand is offered. 'Good morning, Mr. Doherty.'

Clay

I can't bring you to Donegal. I've stood
by my parents' grave. I can't let you see
this sorrow. Forgive me, I'm a coward.
I've not mourned enough. Were I shedding blood,
it would not pay back – the leaves from the trees
in the garden last winter. It was still hard,
it will always be hard. Mother, father,
the grave opens, it will never close.
I'm telling these secrets to a stranger.
They'd love him, the cut of him, his smiles, his clothes.
August, October, I'm frightened of the fall.
Forgive me, I cannot bring you to Donegal.

Frank McGuinness *The Stone Jug*